3-3-06

To my friend Lillian,

Warm regards and
we are so blessed to
know you and call you
friend.
May God bless
you always,

GO | Russillan

THE BIRTH OF AN ARTIST

A JOURNEY OF DISCOVERY

ED HAMILTON

Chicago Spectrum Press
Louisville, Kentucky 40207

CHICAGO SPECTRUM PRESS
4824 BROWNSBORO CENTER
LOUISVILLE, KENTUCKY 40207
502-899-1919

Printed in the U.S.A.

10 9 8 7 6 5 4 3 2 1

ISBN: 1-58374-130-5
        978-1-58374-130-6

The "chop" used to introduce chapters in this book is made up of Ed Hamilton's initials. He imprints this chop in all his clay models before they are cast.

ACKNOWLEDGMENTS

I could not have written this book without the person who has lived these events with me and served as my typist, proofreader, part-time editor, memory jogger, and lifetime confidante, Bernadette Hamilton. We have journeyed hearts and hands together for 38 years, since August 12, 1967. We have faced the trials of living with a mother-in-law, loss of a child at birth, and death of elders we loved. We have enjoyed our children, each commission and award celebration, our friends and families. I know we will continue together as long as we live because our love for each other makes us love living. Each day is a journey to be traveled—good, bad, or indifferent.

Juanita L. White, educator and writer, and LaVerne Shumake Dunning, genealogist and researcher of family history, laid the groundwork for my story's human elements. Their genealogical research and Juanita's proofreading of revised manuscripts from 2002 to 2005 was invaluable. Their extra effort provided the closure needed to end a mystery and begin a relationship. Juanita has been more than a friend and her tireless and willing effort to read drafts and suggest rewrites has made this book what it is today. She helped me tell the truth and nothing less.

A special thanks to Victoria Brown, our Ms. Vickie, educator and writer now residing in New York, for sitting down with Bernadette and me in 1985. She was the first person to encourage us to record our artistic journey. She was convinced that we had a story that needed to be told. None of us realized that it could not be told until I had found my truth.

Thanks to Frank X. Walker, writer, poet, and educator. He visited my studio over several months while I worked on the sculpture of York. He wrote a book of poems entitled, *Buffalo Dance, the Journey of York* and his words added to my visual representation of York. Frank is on staff at Eastern Kentucky University in Richmond, Kentucky.

Thanks to Kimberly Henderson and Gwendolyn Thompson of LiveLines Editing for providing editing assistance in 2003.

Thanks for their faith and support to Father Richard Fowler, Frank Longaker, Phyllis Krantz, Jane Morton Norton, Norman Kohlhepp, Ming Dick, Martin Sweets, and Jasper Ward, all now deceased. Special thanks to the editorial guidance, encouragement, assistance, and knowledge of Dorothy Kavka.

This book is my best effort to tell my journey of discovery. For any name not mentioned, if you played a major role in my journey as an artist, I thank you.

FOREWORD

Ed Hamilton's life and work are a living testimony to the creative and artistic spirit of master artists of traditional Africa. Ed's art speaks with such clarity, sensitivity, and purpose that it is obvious that he is not on this artistic journey alone. This man from such humble beginnings answered the "call" to a lifelong commitment to artistic creation.

While Ed's youth had its share of pain and loss, it was also filled with lifetime friends and the riches that matter, such as extended family, love in abundance, and community. It was this existence that helped to prepare him for the artistic creations that flow through his mind, heart, and hands.

As brilliant and knowledgeable as he is in artistic techniques and processes, he still could not make the art he makes alone. Even in the solitude and isolation of his studio, Ed Hamilton is never alone because he is a keeper of the culture that stands on the shoulders of elders and ancestors. It is the spirits of the ancestors that communicate with him during these times of creation and help chart his artistic vision while permeating every aspect of his life. You cannot be in a serious conversation with Ed Hamilton for any period of time without him making some meaningful reference to the recent or ancient past. His knowledge of self extends from the Commonwealth of Kentucky to the terra-cottas of Nok and the bronzes of Benin.

He accepts with humility the blessing and challenge of being a part of the African continuum as reflected in African American artistic excellence. His ever-growing knowledge of traditional African and other non-Western aesthetics complements his academic training and gives a deeper meaning to his art and life.

He can see clearly the artistic ancestors on whose shoulders he stands—African American giants in sculpting like Sargent Claude Johnson, Augusta Savage, Edmonia Lewis, and Richmond Barthe. He is equally inspired by the work of living legends like Elizabeth

Catlett, Melvin Edwards, Martin Puryear, Barbara Chase-Riboud, and Richard Hunt.

The outstanding work of Ed Hamilton marks the landscape of the United States of America in a way that goes beyond the mere concept of public art. Ed not only wants to make quality art, he wants to share knowledge, give hope, and lift the human spirit. Wherever Ed places a work of art, it seems to become a special place, a sacred place charged with energy, beauty, and healing balm for a nation. We in the African American arts community view Ed Hamilton's public art as cultural pyramids in urban settings.

May the spirit of the ancestors continue to speak to and through artist Ed Hamilton.

—Willis Bing Davis
Chair, Board of Directors
National Conference of Artists

INTRODUCTION

There are many parts to this story that have played out in the town of my youth. There are many roads that I could have taken. One wrong turn could have taken me to the brink of disaster or failure with a life unfulfilled, like so many others that have had their dreams deferred.

I am consumed by the material that I take from the earth, that substance we know as clay. As I breathe life into the inanimate souls I sculpt of those who still live or who have gone on to their glory, I am a slave to the clay. Could it be that the concrete jungles of my hometown held influence over my future muses?

Before there was a Spirit of Freedom Memorial, a Booker T. Washington Memorial Plaza, or an Amistad Memorial, there has always been the goal and the quest to find another commission to keep the studio alive. As the old saying goes "the beat goes on," and the expenses of keeping a studio going is a never ending task.

One of the major commissions to come from 543 South Shelby Street, in Louisville, Kentucky, has been the African American Civil War Memorial at 10th and U Street NW in Washington, DC, a city of unending memorials. How you find out about these commissions is as much a part of my story as the journey itself.

When you work on public sculptures you are always thinking that this, the one you are presently working on, is the one that will bring you that much closer to fame and fortune. Well, my friend that is not always the case. Each public work takes on a life of its own, and owing to its place in history and the timing of events, there is just no way of knowing how the present or the next commission will impact the public emotionally or financially.

It's at this time in my life that I look back just for a brief moment to try and understand how this journey has taken me from the concrete sidewalks of my beloved old Walnut Street in Louisville, Kentucky, to the intersections of many major cities and beyond. I know my life has taken many twists and turns while I was searching for a sense of identity. Through my journey of self-discovery and as I developed sculpting as my life's work, I have been fulfilled beyond my wildest dreams.

There are times when I am amazed with the process of creating art. I have asked myself, "Where did it all begin, and what were the events that led me to become involved in a profession that can, at times, be like riding on a roller coaster?" I have wondered just what was it that prepared me for a career as an artist and sculptor. Is it a gift from God, is it something in my genes, or is it an element of fate?

This is the journey of Edward N. Hamilton, Jr., who grew up in Louisville during the nineteen-fifties to become a husband, a father, and an artist. I became a sculptor of monuments. Within the last three years, 2002 to 2005, a profound epiphany has taken place in my life. I found out that there is another mother out there who for fifty-seven years has worried about me, prayed for me, and wondered about my life.

I begin the story of my journey with remembrances of my youthful days on Walnut Street, now Muhammad Ali Boulevard, during a time long gone but not forgotten.

CONTENTS

*Early Mammoth
Building, corner of 6th
and Walnut Street,
c.1940s (University of
Louisville
Photographic Archives)*

GROWING UP ON
WALNUT STREET

GROWING UP ON WALNUT STREET

On the banks of the Ohio River lies a Kentucky town called Louisville, the place that I call home, the only home I have known. Louisville, like most other cities, was racially segregated during the 1950s and 1960s.

My part of the world began on Walnut Street at 6th, a magical thoroughfare and place for me. My father, mother and I lived in a three-story apartment building at the corner of 7th and Walnut. I still think of old Walnut Street, now Muhammad Ali Boulevard, as it stretched from 6th all the way down to 18th Street. It was a place that I will always have fond memories of.

Looking east on Walnut Street, 1942 (Photographic Archives, Ekstrom Library)

This was the heart of the Negro community in Louisville during this period of Jim Crow in Kentucky. In its heyday—during the 1930s, 1940s, and 1950s—my street was the mecca of cultural life for Louisville's African Americans.

The block had a personality; it was alive and warm. It could be hypnotic and yet become robust and boisterous. In between time, it could become quiet, sleeping off the pleasures of the week to recharge itself, getting ready for the next new day. This was my street, and I owned every crack and every weed in those concrete sidewalks and I left memories that marked my place in history on those sidewalks. I have left written messages and I carry memories of flesh left behind from scraped knees and elbows, and forehead bruises as a result of my favorite pastime, roller skating.

Most but not all of the businesses, nightclubs, restaurants, movie houses, liquor stores, pawn shops, insurance companies, drug stores, groceries, vegetable markets, barbershops, taxi stands, and beauty shops were either owned or run by African Americans and lined both sides of the street. Walnut Street was the realm of the well-to-do African Americans, the lawyers, doctors, dentists, educators, pastors, and businessmen. The building where our family tailoring and barbershop business was located, the Mammoth Life and Accident Insurance Company, was known as the Gold Coast. You could live and have office space in the building. Several professionals worked and lived in the building.

I was deeply impacted by the sights, smells, and sounds of my neighborhood. Three-dimensional objects stood out to me as if they were a part of my inner spirit and soul. Buildings and architectural statues were a source of amazement that I had to study up close in order to gain a personal perspective. The neon signs and even the department store display windows that lined the shopping district of Fourth Street intrigued me.

I was always fascinated with the vivid realism of the over life-size bronze statue of Abraham Lincoln at the main branch of the public library on 4th and York Streets. As a child, I remember rubbing his feet and looking up and seeing how big he was, and wondering to myself if I could grow this large? I would stand there and contemplate what was he doing with his hands crossed, standing there like an Egyptian statue. Maybe he was standing guard over the library.

I also was interested in looking at the whiskey ads in the liquor store windows because they had three-dimensional plaster busts of some of the liquor products that were named after real people. Something about those busts made of white plaster was intriguing to me, although, to this day, I don't really know why.

Visually, the downtown shopping area, known as Fourth Street, a few blocks uptown from my Walnut Street neighborhood, was stimulating and yet it represented another world. As I reflect back, I believe it was due to the fact that all the mannequins in the windows were white. No colored people in those windows. These display models certainly did not look like the people I saw in my neighborhood everyday. In my corner of

Fourth Street corridor, c. 1940s (University of Louisville Photographic Archives)

*The Grand Theatre
(University of
Louisville
Photographic
Archives)*

the world, the only African American images seen were in the advertisements posted in the beauty salons and barbershops.

Many a day I found myself running in and out of the Lyric Theatre and the Grand Theatre which was across the street from my dad's business. As a young boy, I was allowed into the movies free of charge. The proprietors knew my parents and allowed me to come and go as I pleased. One of my reasons for escaping to the theaters during the summer was that the barbershop was always hot and sticky and the theaters were air-conditioned. It was the best place to be on those hot summer days.

I would stay and watch the feature movie of the week two or three times each sitting. Included with the feature were a news update segment and a cartoon. I could even bring my neighborhood friends with me for free.

There was one movie that had a great impact on me, *Carmen Jones,* starring Dorothy Dandridge and Harry Belafonte. There on the big, wide movie screen were people of color who looked just like the people that I saw every day. What a thrill it was to see all those "colored folks" in dramatic roles of respect rather than in roles of servitude. They were acting, but the movements and words were familiar to me. Their actions reminded me of the people I knew. This was the fifties and "colored" people or "Negroes," were not cast as lead characters in Hollywood movies.

I knew Louisville had a lot going on just by the odors that hung so heavy in the air. Every neighborhood had a distinct scent. The east end of town was permeated with the smell of stockyards. Animals were brought in by trains or trucks, then were slaughtered and processed into meat. Beer breweries were located in the west end of town. I loved to smell those hops brewing. I swear there were times while waiting for a bus you could get a nice buzz going. Other neighborhoods held a strong smell of cigarette tobacco, since at one time Louisville had three cigarette factories. Tobacco was a major industry for Kentucky.

One of Louisville's greatest claims to fame is the annual Kentucky Derby. This first leg of the thoroughbred Triple Crown is held on the first Saturday in May. Derby Week caused my street to spring to life for 24 hours each day. Music, laughter, and southern hospitality were in abundance wherever you went. I loved to see

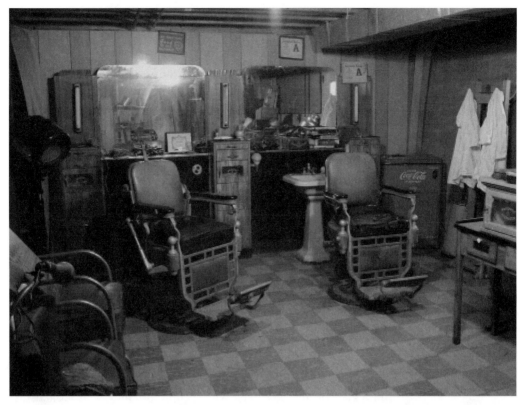

The original barbershop. The complete shop is now in the collection of the Thomas D. Clark Center for Kentucky History, Frankfort, KY, 2005

the long cars being driven up and down Walnut Street while I tried to see some of the faces of famous African Americans coming to town for the Kentucky Derby. During these times, I usually ended up sick from drinking too many soda pops and eating too much.

What fun it was when Dad's business would be full of people getting haircuts, shaves, and their shoes shined. My playmates and I would sneak around the adults, grab a few soda pops and take off running to the back of the shop with our bounty.

My parents were a part of the entrepreneurial spirit of Walnut Street. They owned and operated a tailoring and barbershop called "Your Shop" (later changed to "Your Valet Shop"). Both businesses operated under the same roof in the same space. There were three barber chairs and a six-seat shoeshine stand in the front of the shop. Alterations, cleaning, pressing, and a little pool playing were done in the back.

Dad, Uncle Jack, and associates, c. 1930s-1940s

"Hamp" was my father's nickname and it was said that Hamp and Amy Hamilton owned the most modern cleaner and barbershop on Walnut Street.

*Edward "Hamp"
Hamilton, Sr.,
c.1930s*

*Amy Jane Hamilton,
early 1940s (Evans
Photography)*

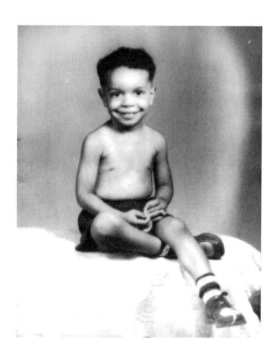

*Ed, Jr., two and a half
years old, 1950
(Gandi Photography)*

As early as 1953, Mama had a barber's license, having trained at Faust O'Bannon Barber School. Mama was the primary barber, along with Ezell Gordon, who cut hair at the shop for many years. Poor Ezell would stand all day cutting hair and at the end of each day, he could hardly walk home since cutting hair and standing all day was not easy on the body, particularly the feet and legs.

It was uncommon for women to become barbers instead of beauticians, but my mama, an independent, strong-willed woman, never let convention hold her back. Her father, Abraham Camp, was her model of an independent businessman. He married Josephine Cummings, and they had a family of four daughters and four sons. Mama was the youngest. In the 1910 census her father was listed as a house carpenter and house owner.

Dad as a soldier, WWI, 1918

My dad was born and raised in Bardstown, Kentucky. His father, Raymond Hamilton, was married to Sudie Doon. They had a family of four sons and three daughters. In the 1900 census, Raymond Hamilton, my grandfather, was listed as a musician.

Edward Norton Hamilton, my daddy, had served in World War I. He left the United States in September, 1918, and landed in Brest, France, off the northwestern coastline of France where he worked in the supply department from August 8, 1918 to May 13, 1919. He was discharged in August, 1919.

Daddy returned to Louisville and worked as a porter, a laborer, and a cleaner and presser after his discharge. The term porter was used for anyone who worked in any business of service and was not restricted to just railroad porters at that time. When he married Mama in 1936, he was 23 years older than she was.

With John J. Sanders he opened Sanders and Hamilton Clothes and Pressers in 1937. I guess you could say that he offered equal opportunity to men and women since he employed Ms. Louise Brown as a presser in that dry cleaning business. Sanders and Hamilton Clothes and Pressers later became Your Shop.

Daddy was the lead tailor. Two of his brothers were also a part of the family business. Uncle Jack shined shoes, and Uncle Charles assisted with the tailoring and dry cleaning.

Six days a week, the business was opened at 7:30 a.m. and closed at 9 p.m. Six days a week, it was a one-stop shop where you could get your clothes cleaned and pressed and a quick shoe

Your Shop, c.1930s.

shine, a shave, a haircut and a manicure, and you were ready for another day. When you walked out the door of 610 West Walnut Street, you were shining from head to toe. I admired the strong sense of pride Daddy and Mama had in running their business. They never missed a day of work. Dad "dressed to the nines" every day, meaning he was never without a tie, a starched shirt, shined shoes, and a hat if he had to leave the shop.

Customers would say, "We can depend on you, Hamp." I remember a sign above the barber section of the shop that read, "If we please you, tell others. If we don't, tell us."

There were always activities going on in the shop, and usually I was in the midst of them. The porters and the waiters who worked downtown in nightclubs or restaurants would come by in the evenings to play pool. When the pool games became intense, Daddy and Mama would keep the shop open longer. One pool player of note was Mr. Gandi, a professional photographer with a studio around the corner on 6th Street, who was quite wild with his pool stick. When his turn came, everyone literally would have to stand back and duck since he had a crazy way of swinging his stick. Many a night, he could have taken out an eye or two of the patrons who ventured too close. When I knew I was safe from Mr. Gandi's antics, I would gather the pool sticks and set the balls and the players would give "Little Biff" (my nickname) a quarter.

I remember many times playing and sleeping in the back of the shop during the day as my parents worked. Most days I was left up to my own devices, which got me in trouble when I would get in Dad's materials and his button boxes. I knew I wasn't supposed to do this, but I found all of his items irresistible. I just couldn't help myself. I was my father's child, and I always loved to be in his presence. Early on, he was very involved in politics and quite a few politicians would stop by to chat with him. He was a die-hard Democrat.

Hamp and Biff, 1950

I loved to look at him. He had such a presence about him. His hands especially fascinated me. I would sit on a stool and watch his hands as he wrote or while he was on the sewing machine. I loved to sit and watch his right foot going a mile a minute, making that Singer sewing machine fly. He had such grace.

When Daddy had a few too many libations, Mama would charge me with getting him from the shop to our apartment. I would hold his hand, walk him down the block, and pull him up three flights of stairs. Daddy would follow my lead, and slowly but surely we would make it up those stairs. I felt so big to be able to get this man, who towered over his little boy, up the stairs.

As I got old enough to stay by myself in the apartment, I was given a key to go and come. Mama would make my breakfast, a bowl of oatmeal, and leave it for me to warm up. It took me a long time before I would eat oatmeal as an adult because of my childhood memories of cold, lumpy, stiff oatmeal. I became the original latchkey child when school was over each day, and I would go back to the apartment by myself.

During the summer, I spent most of my days in the shop, or on the school playground around the corner on 6th Street, playing on the block, and roller skating in and out of the crowds on the block. The summers on the block could get awfully hot—too much concrete, with no shade. Then I would wander into the Natural History Museum on York Street, and what few art galleries there were in downtown Louisville.

The nights were even worse. With no breezes blowing in the apartment, we would lay out on the top floor of the building with the window open hoping for a cool wind to blow over us. We would fan ourselves and eat a lot of ice.

One of the best parts of living on the third floor was the stairs. I would ride the banister from the third floor all the way down to the first floor. Lucky for me I held on so tight that I never once fell off. If Mama caught me doing this I would have been in big trouble, so I never let her see me pulling this crazy stunt.

I think Mama had a great vision of me becoming a doctor, and for several Christmases she bought me doctor kits. Although I did enjoy the candy that came with the kits, I never got the message. Instead, I was always coloring, drawing, making objects out of boxes, fixing things, taking things apart, and investigating how things were created. It's a wonder she didn't want me to become an engineer. Mama never tried to squelch my creativity, but I don't think she understood why I preferred to tear up stuff in her house and at the shop rather than play doctor.

Walnut Street was not without its dark side. I remember one incident that was chilling. It was a warm summer night and I had been down to the ice cream parlor. I was probably around 10 or 11 years old at the time. As I was walking past one row of buildings, I saw a man arguing and fighting with a woman. I could hear her screams as she fought back, and I recall that he gazed over his shoulder and looked out at me. My first reaction was to stand there and keep looking, but there was something about the way he looked at me that quickly got my legs moving and I ran back to the shop. Unfortunately, this was something that happened on the block from time to time. It was not unusual to hear the adults talking about people that were cut or shot in the night. I had seen blood on the sidewalks before, but I had never seen the victims. I had dreams about that incident for quite sometime.

Life on the block was not always easy even looking through a child's eyes. You learn to take the good with the bad. The nightclubs were filled with people laughing, talking and dancing; add a mix of alcohol with the blues blasting on jukeboxes, and a lot of people's dreams became deferred. I could understand why Mama and Daddy were strict with me.

My fondest memories of my father include going with him to boxing and wrestling matches and Roller Derby exhibitions at the old Louisville Armory on the corner of 6th and Walnut. But, as the years progressed, Daddy grew ill with heart disease and was unable to go to sporting events with Mama and me. One April night in 1960, I begged and pleaded with Mama to take us to a roller derby. She finally said yes and off we went. Now that I look back I'm sorry that we went, because otherwise we would have been home when my dad became ill. I couldn't wait to get back home to tell him about the event, and when we arrived, I ran into his bedroom to awaken him. I thought he was just sleeping and shook him several times before I called my mother. We realized he had died while we were gone. I was thirteen years old.

In those days, it was an African American tradition to have the wake in the family's home. It was strange to see Daddy lying in a casket in the dining room for three days. Neighbors and friends visited and expressed their sorrow. I kept wishing that it was a dream and that he would wake up, but it was not a dream.

It was a sad time, since I was an only child and I loved my father very much. There was a void in my life. I would wear Daddy's World War I army trench coat when I wanted to feel connected to him. My extended family, my aunts and uncles, became very important to me.

Mama was even more protective after Daddy's death. If I sneezed, it was off to the doctor's office and how could I forget that tablespoonful of cod liver oil every morning?

I had to wear an asafetida bag, a bad smelling gum resin of oriental plants of the carrot family used as a general prophylactic against disease, pinned to my T-shirt to "ward off germs." I wasn't the only child wearing that sticky bag. Others in my class wore theirs like necklaces. Asafetida came in a little box purchased from the drug store and looked like a stick of chewing gum, but it smelled like bad garbage. Mama would wrap it in a piece of old T-shirt or stocking and pin it near my throat. I probably didn't catch a cold because the smell ran people away. Yet, other than an occasional sore throat, I had no major illness or allergy.

We attended Broadway Temple African Methodist Episcopal Church where Mama was active with the Deaconess Board. Broadway Temple seemed huge when I was young but, in reality, it was only big in my child's mind.

Urban renewal in the 1960s closed my parent's shop and all other major African American businesses in that corridor of Walnut Street. It was a major blow to African American social and cultural life. People lost jobs because businesses decided not to reopen in a different location, or owners decided to take the money and retire, since the price of relocation was expensive. The close community of professionals disappeared quickly. The unity of ownership and self-pride disappeared under the promised newness of urban renewal.

Mama opened another barbershop in the west end of the city. She was older, in her sixties, and her clients decreased. She became a dinosaur in her craft by not adapting to the new style of haircuts for men. She remained open for two to three years before eventually closing the shop in 1975 and retiring. Her barbering chairs and equipment were stored in the basement of our home. Every time I would go to the basement and see all the things that were in the shop, I would imagine I was back on Walnut Street again.

Although all the places that I played as a child are now merely parking lots, my childhood memories remain strong. Sometimes a certain sight, sound, smell, would bring back the memory of the eateries and the bars with music. The whiff of alcohol in the air or the scent of hair being straightened with pomades will take me back to the Walnut Street of my youth.

I never got everything I thought I wanted, but I had everything I needed including the love it takes to raise a child. It was a community that cared and, unlike today, people looked out for each other because we were all together in that segregated neighborhood. We worked for ourselves to make the ends meet. There was dignity among the people on Walnut Street. I realize now that even back then the people of color had lives filled with hopes and dreams. Yet, without a sense of hope, without a sense of family or a steady income, one could get lost in the abyss and lost to history forever. Due to the progress known as urban renewal, which I called urban removal, only the sidewalks remain. Everything else is just a memory of a time and places gone by—the ghosts of the buildings, the phantom people, all are quiet and all are gone. There is nothing but dust and parking lots and a lot of fond memories that flash back from time to time to haunt me.

Ed at easel in
Shawnee High School
art class, 1965

SCHOOL DAYS,
ART DAYS

SCHOOL DAYS, ART DAYS

It was in 1958 that Mama and Daddy moved us from our three-room apartment at 7th and Walnut Streets. They saved enough money and built a new home down in the west end of Louisville known as the Parkland area. I entered Parkland Junior High School, an integrated school, where my artistic talents were discovered. My art teacher, Harriet O'Malley, planted and watered the seed. Ms. O'Malley called my mother and said, "I think Ed's got something and I want to help him develop it." Even in my early teens, she told my mother that art should be my vocation.

Under her tutelage I blossomed. She was a great art teacher, always pushing her students towards various media. It was through her that I started attending the Louisville Children's Free Art Classes at the Art Center School. Little did I realize this place later would be the college I would attend.

The seed was planted and now my art teacher at Shawnee High School, Ms. Patsy Griffith, also allowed my abilities to grow. Admittedly, high school was not one of my favorite places. It was the beginning of total integration in the city schools of the Louisville public school system. Some white teachers and white students were not ready for integration and I felt as though I were living in two different worlds, white by day and Negro by night. I still remember the animosity and disrespect from some white students and adults in that school.

But some teachers were able to move past the issue of color and Patsy Griffith was one of those teachers. She took me under her wing and taught me a great deal about technique and art history. Ironically, my early paintings and sketches were of white people because that was all I saw in classroom textbooks and public artwork throughout Louisville.

Patsy encouraged me to apply for a scholarship to the Art Center School in Louisville and worked unceasingly with me to develop my portfolio. From the essays about the impressionist painters, to

Parkland Junior High, 1960

Auguste Rodin, the great 19th century Parisian sculptor, to the pencil sketches and tempera paintings I completed, she made sure the breadth and depth of my skills were represented. The result was a four-year scholarship to the Art Center School located near the University of Louisville campus.

During my senior year in 1965 at Shawnee High School, I was named "The Friendliest" in my graduating class. Even though I had not consciously centered on being accepted, I was honored to receive this title of recognition from my classmates.

I was somewhat of a geek, complete with big, black, horn-rimmed glasses, pencils and pens in my pocket, and slicked-down hair, parted on the side. I was already trying to be an artist at this point, but it would take another four years to be able to say that this was what I wanted to do as my life pursuit.

High school, voted friendliest in class (1965 yearbook photo)

I started my collegiate career at the Art Center School. My major was painting and graphic arts. Although I was successful, my heart wasn't fully committed to painting. One day while at my easel I was on a roll, just laying down the paint on a water scene. The director of the Art Center School, Nell Peterson, was showing a group of patrons around the school.

For some strange reason, she leaned over my shoulder and asked me if I had ever seen the ocean. I told her that I had not and she responded, "Well, how can you paint something that you have never seen?" I put my brushes down to ponder her question. Well, I thought, how could students painting abstract subjects know what abstraction looks like? Has anybody ever seen abstraction?

After hearing her insult, a man on the tour came over to me and said, "Pay no attention to what she said. You just keep painting. You're doing OK." That was Norman Kohlhepp, a painter, sculptor, engineer, and world traveler. He would later give the school the money to create a foundry for bronze sculpting in the back court yard of the Art Center School.

Students were not allowed to take sculpting classes until their sophomore year. It was when I walked into the sculpture studio that I caught the sculpting fever. I saw modeling tools and smelled the clay. I felt an inner glow that spread throughout my body.

Somehow I knew sculpting would allow me to use all my creative energies and I was hooked.

Sculpture to me was physical. It had dimension. An artist can't fake form in three-dimensions. Suddenly it all made sense and clicked perfectly with the way I viewed objects.

I said, "To hell with paint." I let my brushes get hard because painting just didn't do it for me anymore.

My sculpting teacher, Alan Paulson, was an outstanding teacher. Although he sculpted in wood, he allowed students to explore all the avenues of sculpture: stone and wood carving, mold making, and welding. Such exposure allowed us to define ourselves as artists in the medium for which we had the strongest passion.

Our greatest experience and joy was when we, the students, built the bronze foundry on school grounds. The foundry was the

high point of art school for me. The furnace was built to withstand temperatures from 1900 to 2000 degrees. The furnace and the crucible would rumble and roar and the ground would shake as the force of air and gas came through the two inch round pipes whenever we melted bronze ingots, or any other scrap metal. We melted anything that we would get our hands on, even lead pipes. It reminded me of Rodin's sculpture, *The Gates of Hell*, which includes bodies swirling in a vast underworld of intense heat, a Dante's Inferno. It was as close to hell as anyone of us would ever want to get as we poured the melted bronze into the molds to cast a student's sculpted artwork. We would watch that hot, molten metal run like water into the red-hot ceramic molds that sat deep in the sandpits. It was exciting to feel the ground rumble and feel the heat of the fur-

The Art Center School with Ed's first direct plaster life-sized figure, 1969

nace when we had our pouring. This usually took place at night, and after the pour, a six pack of cold beer sure did taste good as we stood around, hot, sweaty, and pleased with what we had just accomplished.

Clay modeling, bronze casting, and mold making were exciting, comfortable, and challenging to me. I spent my time trying to make the best molds. No object was too complicated to figure out a way to mold and cast. I can truly say that I never miscast a bronze piece during our foundry time at school. There were times when I would help others to make sure that their bronzes would come out correctly.

I was very influenced by Rodin's figurative, classical style, and read and studied every book on him that I found in the school library. I learned from reading about him that light is important when modeling figures. His modeling of life models, real people, allowed the viewer to visibly see the muscles and energy in the figures when they were complete.

Because I sculpt the body before I put any clothes on the figure, the muscles and body structure beneath the clothing can be visualized, which gives the sculpted figures form and life.

I also learned to weld metal and turn it into sculptural forms. The discovery of the works of welder and abstract sculptor, David Smith of Bolton Landing, New York, opened my eyes and spirit to free-form sculptures.

The Art Center School provided me with four years of camaraderie and schooling. I had found a community of like minds and creative soul mates. Somewhere between the two worlds, of figurative and abstract, I would discover my own muse.

Bernadette Chapman
Hamilton, 1980

LOVE IS IN THE AIR

LOVE IS IN THE AIR

All my life I've loved and had a great deal of respect for women. A lady's man? You bet. Big, tall, short, and small, women have always been a special part of my life.

Between the ages of 11 and 12 years old I became acutely aware of the magnetism of the opposite sex. At five o'clock every afternoon, I would position myself on the second floor stairwell of our building, the Mammoth Life Insurance Company, and watch the beautiful African American women leave work, all dignified and pretty, always an eyeful. Those who knew me would smile and say, "Hi, Biff. What are you doing?" I loved their attention.

In my young adulthood, there was always a young lady for me to wine and dine, but it was never anything serious, just a good date. That changed in the winter of 1967 when I saw Bernadette Sonja Chapman walking through the "Sub," a public cafeteria on the campus of the University of Louisville. I didn't know what real love was all about until I met her.

Bernadette was a student at the university, and the Art Center School was housed just up the street. For African American students, who were very much in the minority, the Sub was *the* place to congregate.

This particular day, it must have been meant for me to see her, as I happened to take a break from class and ventured over to the Sub as she came through the door, high heels clicking across the tile floor. When I saw Bernadette, I was immediately smitten and transfixed as she walked past me. I turned and looked and asked one of her friends, Sharon Clark, a childhood friend of mine, "Who is she?" Her reply was "That's Bernadette."

Well, the name alone was enough for me. I wanted to know this sultry, young female with a fine, brown frame. Now there I was, standing covered in plaster and linseed oil, pencils and pens protruding from my pocket and black horn-rimmed glasses sliding down my nose. Looking like that, I couldn't approach her and introduce myself without a little help. So I had one of her female friends do the honors.

Bernadette didn't seem very impressed with me that day, but she did agree later to give me her telephone number. I was persistent, calling regularly. Finally, I got up enough nerve to ask her out to a dance on campus, and she said yes. I think she thought I was still going to be seedy and smelling like linseed oil and plaster.

I fooled her. When I pulled up to the door, I was sharp as a tack, smelling good, and feeling good. I dressed in a suit and tie and brushed my hair back. My father would have been proud of the way I looked. She gave me an approving, albeit shocked, look, and we headed for the dance. When she found out I could talk *and* dance, I guess she was more at ease.

Courting days, 1966

Bernadette is the oldest of eight children, four brothers (Caldwell "Mingtoi," Michael, Stephen, and John "Johnny") and three sisters (Betty C. Strasser (Eric), Cardell C. Smith (Benny), and Deborah C. Hampton. They lived with her mother, Agnes Gentry Chapman, stepfather, John Board, step-grandfather, James Bishop, and her grandmother, Anna Elizabeth Bishop.

Ms. Bishop was a true southern, Christian lady whom we fondly called Granny. Granny was the matriarch of the family. Whenever I visited her house, there was always a big spread of food and it seemed that I was always hungry. I remember the large can of lard, the shortening used for frying food back in the 1950s and 1960s, which sat in the kitchen. I ate many a fried chicken and Friday night fish dinner cooked with the lard from that can. Sunday dinner was always a feast.

They all lived in a big house, 4642 West Broadway, located two houses before the floodwall and across a dead-end street from Shawnee Park. I could constantly see the family concept of love for each other. Everyone pitched in together in that family. You had three adults working to feed a family of twelve, and a grandmother who watched over them all. There was a lot of love and laughter there.

Bernadette's great-aunt, Agnes Ford, was also an instrumental part of the family though she didn't live with them. She had no children but she lived in Louisville and provided friendship and love to her great-nieces and great-nephews.

On our wedding day, with Bernadette's stepfather, John Board

The family, to me, embodied the concept of using a village to raise children. I learned about sharing and caring from watching their interactions with one another as brothers and sisters. Like most large families they had a rhythm and hum that resonated with interactions and reactions. I observed the same responses in families of relatives and friends. Everyone had chores and played together, but like any family, they would enjoy each other for awhile, and then there would be times when they would dislike the company of one another. But disputes didn't last long and verbal or physical fights were quickly forgiven or forgotten because of their rule, "Kiss each other on the lips before the incident is considered settled."

I love large families. Deep down, I would always wonder to myself what it would be like to have brothers and sisters. It could get quite lonely when I would return home from visiting friends and relatives, just me and my room.

As the relationship grew serious, Bernadette's grandmother told her, "You better grab that boy. That boy loves you." What really sealed the deal? Bernadette caught the flu during our courtship, and I sent her a dozen red roses. That did it!

We went together for about six months and married on August 12, 1967. My mom was quite upset that I was doing this. She really did not approve. I told her that I loved Bernadette and that I was getting married in spite of this disapproval. My mama and Bernadette's mother were concerned about the fact that we were young and had not experienced life. We informed them that we would travel and learn about life together. We did not see this as an ending for us because we were in love, we were expecting a baby, and we had all the confidence in the world that we could make our marriage work. Our son, Edward N. Hamilton, III, was born in 1968. We hoped he would be a New Year's Day baby, but the delivery was long and he was born on January 2, 1968.

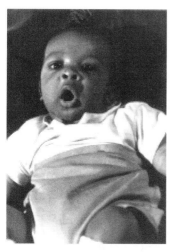

Edward N. Hamilton, III, 1968 (photo by Dennis Christoff)

Bernadette and I discussed the reasons why we should or should not have more children. We married young and the efforts of raising a son, balancing part-time and full-time jobs, establishing my art career, attending art school classes day or night for me, and university classes at night after work for Bernadette were challenging for both of us. We discussed increasing our family using all the reasons young couples do for not having more children—low finances, not the right time, career moves, and let's wait until after this or after that.

We talked about having the ideal American number of two children, hopefully a boy and a girl. As time passed, we decided we wanted two children no matter what sex they were.

In 1974, with our biological clocks ticking, my response was not a firm commitment. I was passive and nonchalant about having another child because I was an only child and I had survived without brothers and sisters. Eddie, nicknamed "Munch," was now eight years old and Bernadette had graduated with her elementary teaching degree from the University of Louisville.

In 1975, Bernadette was working as a third grade teacher at Valley Elementary School. She finally said, "We will try for the second baby." Five months later she was pregnant with our second child and we both were happy.

She began to have problems during the third month of her pregnancy. It started with her complaining of pain in her abdomen, which was diagnosed as a cyst that was filled with fluid on one ovary. One day, while she was at work, she had to leave her classroom and rushed to the bathroom. She told me after she arrived home that she had vomited in the bathroom after a sharp pain in her stomach. She had no other symptoms and by then she was feeling fine. After she visited the doctor, it was determined that the cyst had burst. Everything was great.

On May 13, 1976, after a Mother's Day brunch with the family, Bernadette noticed that there was little to no movement from the baby. The next day she began to spot blood. We went to the hospital and our baby son of seven months was stillborn. It was traumatic because we wanted this second child. He had been named and loved in our hearts. We were told that the weight of the baby caused the placenta to break away, resulting in the miscarriage.

Bernadette was gospel Baptist and I was African Methodist Episcopal. We were both active in our churches, but we needed a church that met both our needs. Our son Edward was two years old and we were feeling the guilt of not having one church home for the family. One weekend, we were sitting on the porch of our apartment building and Father Charles Tachau, the vicar of St. George Episcopal Church, walked by. He started talking to us, since he was canvassing the neighborhood for new church members. We attended a Sunday service and it has been our church home since 1969. Eddie and Kendra were baptized at St. George's.

Bernadette and I took on a series of jobs to make ends meet. While I was in college, I worked as a busboy and waiter at a private club. Our plan was for me to graduate first and begin teaching, since I had only two years left to earn a degree. Ironically, some of the people I served at this private club later became my patrons.

I also worked for an ammunition plant on the graveyard shift from 12 a.m. to 7 a.m. in Charlestown, Indiana, earning $100 a week. I took the job because we were looking toward happiness with better finances and made all the plans young couples make when you have a weekly paycheck. I was saving money for a new Volkswagen Beetle—Bernadette did not drive and I convinced her that this was the best car to have for gas mileage and safety. We wanted to move out of our one bedroom apartment with the bathroom down the hall that we shared with another tenant on the second floor of a two-story single family home.

Bernadette and I discussed how this would play out with me going to school during the day and working at night. It meant I could help with family finances and have money for art supplies. She did not want me to forget the big picture of getting my degree, and our plan was that after I finished my degree, she would go back and finish her degree.

I am not a night person. We usually were in the bed by 10 p.m. I was still on a 90 day probation at the plant, where I would stamp USA on the seal of the artillery shells that came down a conveyor belt. I had a break scheduled for 15 minutes after two hours of work. I noticed when it came time for me to take my break that my fellow worker had extended hers. Finally, I was able to go outside and I sat by the building enjoying a cool summer breeze. The next thing I knew someone kicked the bottom of my shoe. I had fallen asleep and like Rip Van Winkle, feeling as I woke up, it was an entire new era.

My supervisor asked me, "Where is your badge?"

I replied, "It's right here." I reached for the spot on my shirt where it was supposed to be and it was gone. He had taken the badge from my shirt while I slept and informed me that I was fired for sleeping on the job. I was a week away from completing my probation period.

Needless to say, I went home with a sad face. When Bernadette came home from work I said, "Guess what?"

She looked at me for a moment and said, "You got fired."

I replied, "Yes." We looked at each other for a while and began to laugh. She never criticized me for not being the major contributor to our household expenses. She once told me that because I went to work everyday never knowing whether I would make a sale or not she believed in me and that my future was not with a 9 to 5 job in corporate America.

I've always considered our home my shelter from the world. No matter how bad life is, I can always come home and be accepted.

My next job was creating illustrations for a home improvement store. Every week, I would buy a pack of Swisher Sweets cigars at the liquor store across the street from where I worked in order to cash my paycheck. I would walk more than a dozen blocks to a drugstore to buy a case of infant formula for my son Eddie. Because the buses ran slow on the weekend, it was a lot easier to walk than wait for the bus. Sometimes a person could wait from 30 minutes to an hour at a bus stop.

At various times, Bernadette worked as a keypunch operator at a local census bureau, a bank secretary and teller assisting with small business loans, and a legal secretary. During this time, she was working full-time and attending U of L at night to finish her degree in elementary education.

I would take her to work, pick her up afterwards, and take her to a 5:15 p.m. class. While she was in class, I would pick up three-year old Eddie from Granny's, and work on projects in our dining room while Eddie ate, slept, or played nearby. With Eddie in his car seat, I would go and pick Bernadette up at U of L by 6:35 p.m. This would happen two to four times a week depending on my wife's schedule.

In 1969, we saved the $500 for the down payment on a new beige Volkswagen Beetle for which we paid $55 a month. I taught her to drive a year later. She panicked on the hills because the Volkswagen was a stick shift and would roll back as she pressed on the gas and eased off the clutch. One time she even got out of the car on a hill and I had to take over. Driving a stick shift was not easy for her in the beginning. Over time, she got the hang of it and could boogie down the highways.

I graduated in 1969 from the Art Center School and Bernadette graduated from the University of Louisville in 1975. Persistence paid off. It was through the grace of God and the support of family and friends that we were able to accomplish all that we did during those years.

Eddie and Kendra, 1980

Kendra was born on August 3, 1977; there is a ten year difference in our children's ages. Eddie doted on his little sister. We said that sugar couldn't melt in her mouth as far as he was concerned.

The children are creative. Eddie graduated with a degree in culinary arts from Jefferson Community College, moving to Orlando, Florida, after receiving an internship with Walt Disney World in 1986. He stayed there for about eight years, and still lives and works in Orlando. My son meets no strangers and is a true people-person and those who know him just absolutely love him.

When Kendra was a little girl, I used to bring her to the studio Monday through Friday after her one-half day in Montessori School. I bought her a drawing desk, and she would sit and do drawings until I would take her to Granny's house for baby-sitting. She liked to draw and was good at building things. She helped me build a deck and a screened-in porch for our house. She probably should have considered being an engineer.

Kendra really found herself in music. She took Suzuki violin and French horn lessons and ultimately received a partial college scholarship because of her musical talent. Kendra received a business and marketing degree from Kentucky State University in 2002.

Kendra, Eddie, Ed, and Bernadette, 1998

Neither of our children is looking to make a living in the arts. They have had a taste of what I do, and they have seen the pain and suffering I endured for the sake of my career. I didn't try to influence them to become artists. I just wanted them to experience a variety of things and be who they wanted to be. Whatever they didn't want to do, we didn't pressure them to do.

They are their own people. Bernadette and I are very satisfied that we raised good children who have never been in trouble a day in their lives. It indeed takes a village to raise a child; Granny, who died in November, 1981, was our main help.

My family has kept me grounded and helped me to achieve my goals and together we help each other. Without such support, life's long and short-term goals are harder to achieve. We discuss the pros and cons of art projects, family issues, and any factor that could impact the harmony of our family. In my wife's and my many roles as parents, husband and wife, or as friends, we talk about situations and select alternatives that best meet the needs of all involved. Decisions have been good and bad, but Bernadette and I have always accepted responsibility for our actions and reactions. Bernadette is now Director of the Optional, Magnet, and Advance Programs with the Jefferson County Public Schools.

*The Louisville Art
Workshop, 35th and
Del Park Place, 1969*

MY FOUNDATION:
THE LOUISVILLE ART WORKSHOP

MY FOUNDATION:
THE LOUISVILLE ART WORKSHOP

Friends are important. My friends included a group of people experiencing the same ups and downs, the same problems of trying to make a living from art when no one was buying. We participated in the same exhibits and did not sell anything.

I have firm bonds with friends who have traveled the hard road to artistic success with me and who knew me when we were all working toward being successful as artists. We cried together, ate together, partied together, and raised children together. We have all moved in different directions, but we stayed in touch.

Long before my muse would take me on my life's journey of sculpting, a group of artists had an overwhelming effect on my life. The year was 1969 and Alfred Phillips and I were graduating from the Art Center School. The showing of our student works was scheduled to run for a week instead of a month, the time graduates normally received, because the art school staff had scheduled a traveling art exhibit from Chicago during our graduation exhibition. Thus, we lost three weeks from our scheduled month.

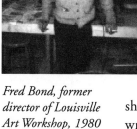

Crushed, I looked around the gallery and wondered who would see the works I had created. I was looking for feedback and I didn't know where to find an answer. Through a conversation with my sculpture instructor, Alan Paulson, a woodcarver, I learned that there was a group of African American artists in the west end of Louisville who might be able to help. I was an African American student graduating from a four year accredited art school, but I had to turn to the African American community to properly showcase my artistic dreams and talents.

Fred Bond, former director of Louisville Art Workshop, 1980 (photo by Ron Stringer)

That group turned out to be the Louisville Art Workshop, founded in the 1960s by Fred Bond, a ceramist, painter and writer; Dr. Robert Douglas, "Dr. Bob," an art history educator, writer, painter and sculptor; Mervin Aubespin, "Merv," a painter

Past members of the Workshop: (l to r) William Duffy, Ed Hamilton, Merv Aubespin, Eugene Thomas, Dr. Robert Douglas, Robert Holmes, (sitting) G. Caliman Coxe, 1998

and writer, now retired from *The Courier-Journal* newspaper; James High, a painter; and G. Caliman Coxe, "G. C.," a painter and surrogate father to me. A host of other artists, writers, and dancers added a New York SoHo air that I desperately needed. As a young artist, I learned from these people that there is strength in numbers and I forged a special bond with Fred, Dr. Bob, and G.C.

Fred literally lived at the Workshop with his wife, Anna, a poet, and their family. Fred and Anna were the catalysts who kept the Workshop together. Anna made the Workshop a home, writing poetry and reading her work to students and during exhibits, while sustaining us with her fine cooking and words of wisdom.

Anna Bond, with one of her daughters, 1969

These dedicated artists taught me how to be part of an organization. It was not about any one individual; it was about the Workshop. We were community-based. As a group, we had a lot going on, including creative writing workshops, painting classes, children's art workshops, and dance classes.

Although I learned the mechanics of art at school, I learned the individuality of art from the Workshop. Everything Workshop members had learned throughout the years was shared with young, new artists. It was not elitist. They said, "Hey man, if you've got a talent, we're going to help you hone it." All artists should be as unselfish and giving of their gifts.

Anna Lauderdale Huddleston, a public school art teacher, administrator, and fabric designer, was the strongest female personality in the Louisville Art Workshop. She took no prisoners and refused to let anyone with talent accept being second best. She convinced me to take the position of director of the Louisville Art Workshop in the early 1970s. Due to lack of funding, the Workshop closed permanently in 1973.

G.C., the dean of the black artists of Louisville and a master painter, was teacher, mentor, and friend to all who knew him. He was the glue that held our group together after the Workshop closed. We would meet at his home on Winnrose Way or my studio on Shelby Street and have friendly, sometimes intense critiques of our artwork. Sad to say, since G.C.'s passing in 1999, the remnants of our group don't meet on a regular basis if at all.

Bob Douglas, James High, Merv Aubespin, and I still see each other on a regular basis that is more social than artistic. We meet at Joe's Palm Room, a local jazz nightclub, to celebrate life.

The Courier-Journal & Times, "Arts" section
Sunday, March 12, 1972

HAMILTON AT SPALDING

THE WORK of Edward Hamilton in the Spalding College Gallery represents this able young artist's first one-man show, though he is already a veteran exhibitor in group shows here. At Spalding are works in several media, mostly paintings, prints and sculpture. The show is excellent indication of Hamilton's strengths and weaknesses. His design sense is extremely keen and this shows especially in his prints and sculptures. Apparently Hamilton's greatest need now is production time. Hamilton, a Louisville School of Art graduate, teaches at Iroquois High School and the Louisville Art Workshop and is working toward an art degree at Spalding College. Hamilton has the talent to lick the time problem, however.

–Sarah Lansdell, Art Critic

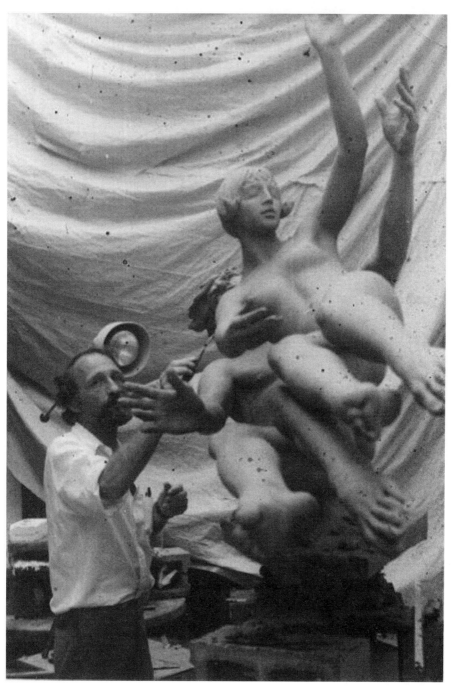

Barney Bright
working on clay model
of Truth and Justice,
1973

THE BRIGHT ERA

THE BRIGHT ERA

Upon graduation from the Art Center School, I found that I could not make a living by painting and sculpting. I held several part-time jobs to make ends meet from 1968 to 1970. One job required me to make signs at night for a general merchandise and clothing store while locked in the building as I worked from 9 p.m. until 7 a.m. Being locked in worried Bernadette. She asked, "What if a fire starts, or a burglary alarm goes off while you are locked in the building?" I was lucky that it never happened, but it worried me also. I did display work during the day for a local department store from 3 p.m. until 8 p.m.

Anna Huddleston, a friend from the Louisville Art Workshop, told me that I needed to teach art. I returned to the University of Louisville to acquire a teaching certificate and my student teaching experience was under her tutelage. In 1970, I started teaching ceramics and sculpture at Iroquois High School as an assistant to Delores Huffman, the painting and graphic arts teacher, while working toward my teaching certification in art through the Career Opportunity Program (COP). This was a job that I truly enjoyed, and which allowed me to devote time to my own artistic endeavors.

I decided that the classroom was the place for me, since I would have a steady income by teaching art in the public schools. Had it not been for a life-changing, chance meeting, I probably would have continued my career as a high school art teacher.

That meeting took place in the spring of 1973. I was buying art supplies for school at a ceramic shop next door to the studio of Barney Bright, the only sculptor in Louisville who was actually making a living from sculpting. I had followed his work through art school and was blown away by the power of one of his sculptures, *Earth Mother*. I had never met him, but I knew of his artistic talent and the strength of his sculptures.

As I was leaving the ceramic shop, I glanced at Barney Bright's door. I should knock on his door and introduce myself, I thought.

I was apprehensive because I thought he would not let me come into his studio. At the time, I had an Afro hairstyle that was three inches high, and dressed in the "superfly" look. I continued to my car, but just as I began turning the key in the ignition, Barney came out to check on his mail. I knew it was now or never. I got out of the car, walked over, and introduced myself.

I love fate. Barney invited me into his studio and my entire life changed. During our conversation, he told me that he had taught night school classes at the Art Center School. While at the school, Barney saw a life-sized plaster rendition of *Adam* by Rodin. He admitted that the rendition was a little rough, but he felt the person who made it had potential. I told him that was my art piece. From that chance meeting, we formed a long-term friendship.

As we sat in his studio filled with wonderful objects he had created, Barney mentioned that he had a major commission coming up and could use some extra help. He asked if I might be available to assist him on several projects. My response was, "Yes, sir." I was ready right then!

I couldn't wait to tell Bernadette that I had met Barney Bright and had been asked to work for him. I also told her that this would be my last year teaching high school art. She wasn't too sure that this was something that I should do, but she believed in me. The entrepreneurial spirit of my parents and my Walnut Street elders kicked in.

Mocking up River Horse *for Barney, 1973*

The decision to become a full-time artist required acceptance, sacrifice, and understanding from both of us. Our medical benefits and a steady income would be handled though Bernadette's job, and my wife attended graduate school on nights and weekends to complete her masters degree in education and Rank I certification which increased her earning potential. Our lives were similar to the corporate husband expanding his career while the wife maintained the home front, but the roles and the finances were in reverse. As the years progressed, my family knew that my work would bring both feast and famine. In the early years, I sacrificed my income to establish a name for myself, yet, during that period, we never wanted for anything. Whenever a major commission was awarded to me, it was time for our feast.

Joining Barney was one of the best decisions that I ever made in my life. Through the early 1970s, I chased bronze using drills and torches to make welded errors disappear and built armatures (the steel, styrofoam, wood, chicken wire, etc. used to hold clay in place) for various projects. I also helped build the main studio where *The River Horse,* and the *Louisville Clock* were dedicated during Louisville's bicentennial celebration in 1976, and Barney's other major commissions were created.

I made most of the wax models and molds for Barney's projects and drove plaster castings and wax models to the Fine Arts Sculpture Centre in Pontiac, Michigan, the casting foundry that Barney used. A fellow friend, former student of the art school, and part-time employee working with Barney, Bill Eastridge, would go with me as did G. C. Coxe because he had a sister living in Detroit. They would help me drive.

The Louisville Clock, *The Fourth Street Mall, Louisville, 1976*

The last major sculpture that I helped Barney complete was *The Louisville Clock.* This was a public sculpture composed of historic figures who would "race" daily at noon. They were engineered to have a different winner each time. The figures included George Rogers Clark, Louis the XVI, Daniel Boone, Thomas Jefferson, and the Belle of Louisville. At the top of *The Louisville Clock* was Zachary Taylor, the former president of the United States; Mary Anderson, a local stage actress and singer; Henry Watterson, a *Courier-Journal* editor; D.W. Griffith, the silent film movie director; and Oliver Cook, a trumpet player and the only African American on the clock. I made the wax patterns and Barney assigned me to take the patterns to the foundry in Pontiac, Michigan. Bill and I loaded up the car and picked up G.C.

Barney stressed that we must keep the air-conditioning on to keep the waxes from melting or changing shape. We were driving Barney's 1972 Chevrolet station wagon and after several hours on the road, the fan belt broke outside of Bowling Green, Michigan. There were no cell phones at that time, and we waited approximately three hours before a state trooper pulled up and called a tow truck. We were towed to a garage where the fan belt was replaced and within two hours we were on our way again. We were lucky that the fan belt broke at night when it was cooler rather

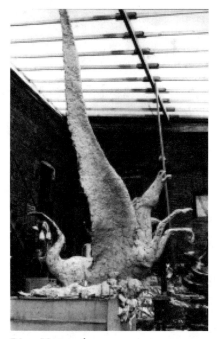

River Horse, *clay model, 1973*

Barney Bright putting on clay for River Horse, *1973*

Ed brushing down the bronze River Horse, *Federal Building, 6th and Chestnut, Louisville, 1974 (photo by Bill Luster,* The Courier-Journal)

than during the heat of the day. Five hours in 90 plus degree heat would have resulted in major repair work to each waxed piece. We arrived with all the waxed pieces holding their original shapes.

After we delivered the waxes, we drove to Detroit. G.C. and I would stay with his sister, Helen Richardson while Bill caught the Greyhound bus from Detroit to Providence, Rhode Island, to visit his family. Then G.C. and I would drive back to Louisville.

I am extremely proud of the fact that Barney allowed me to sign my name on *The River Horse*. This commission, a bronze horse with a fish tail and 20-foot wingspan, resides in front of the Federal Building in downtown Louisville. It is not often that an artist is able to work for an established artist and be allowed to put his name on the completed work. I think it was Barney's way of showing his gratitude for the work and expertise I put forth in assisting him with projects.

My work with Barney opened doors to future patrons and greatly enhanced my skills and knowledge. He provided me with the what, when, where, why, whom, and how of sculpting, writing work contracts, entering competitions, and managing business. It was through his tutelage, friendship, and mentoring that I developed the skills and knowledge to make representational sculptures, or exact likenesses.

I loved working with Barney, and I loved his style. At one point while I was working in clay, however, my figurative sculptures started to look like something from Barney Bright instead of from Ed Hamilton. "Wait a minute," I thought. "I can't do this."

Every artist must have his or her own style, so I had to back off. Through no fault of my mentor, I had to leave Barney's studio to come into my own, to hone a unique style, and to pursue my own commissions.

Our relationship continued after I was able to move into my own studio. I would phone him to come to my studio and take a look at my projects and offer advice.

Barney opened the door of sculpting and I walked through it to become the sculptor that I am today. I hate to think of where and what I would be today had it not been for Barney—probably still teaching high school art, indeed, an honorable profession, but not one I would be happy doing.

Barney was a master craftsman, sculptor and friend. He passed away in 1997 and I miss him very much.

In studio with Aqua
Mother, *1979 (photo
by Richard Carver)*

FINDING MY MUSE

FINDING MY MUSE

When I left my apprenticeship with Barney, I was not alone for long. I found space to use as a studio at 712 W. Main Street in the basement of the former Preservation Alliance building. I brought some of the artists from the Louisville Art Workshop with me. G.C. named the studio "Me, Ed, and Fred." G.C., the elder statesman and the one with the quick wit, was the Me; Fred and I were represented by our first names.

G.C. was working at the Fort Knox Army base as an illustrator. Fred was teaching at various high schools and later took a job as director of the Cincinnati Art Consortium in Cincinnati, Ohio. My friend William Duffy, known as "Duffy" to his art friends, joined us later at the studio. He was working at the Louisville Natural History and Science Museum as an exhibit preparer, directly across the street from the studio.

We practiced our craft in the basement studio, developing our individual styles. I was trained in a traditional method of sculpting and had learned how to create representational work, but there were—and still are—some other energies within me that wanted to come out.

I have no problems going from real form to the abstract. I actually enjoy getting away from a representational piece and working on something that contains elements of form, shape, mass, or design as opposed to developing a face with eyeballs, a nose and mouth, and a body with correct anatomy.

Meanwhile, I continued to paint and experiment with metal and fabricated pieces, while as a studio artist, I continued to look for my muse.

Processional Cross, *bronze, St. Augustine Catholic Church, 1974*

I started sculpting liturgical pieces for Catholic churches as a part of my income. My first liturgical piece was a processional cross commissioned by Father Fischer of St. Augustine Catholic Church when the church was remodeled. The sculpture

The Christ,
plaster,
c. 1976 (photo
by Eddie Davis)

is a bronze statue of Jesus with his arms outstretched as though he is on a cross. It could be interpreted as a crucified or a risen Christ. The piece is approximately two feet tall and is meant to be placed on a six-foot wooden staff, so that in a procession it is eight feet in height. It is housed at St. Augustine Catholic Church, 13th and Broadway, in Louisville. There is a replica of the work at St. George Episcopal Church on the corner of 26th and Virginia Avenue, also in Louisville.

Thanks to meeting C. Robert "Bob" Markert, a stained-glass artist with a studio in the same building as I was in, I was given opportunities to create additional liturgical sculptures for Catholic churches in Louisville and throughout Kentucky. When Bob was commissioned to do stained glass windows or reconfigure a sacred space for a church, he would recommend me, if it seemed appropriate, to design a tabernacle or other pieces to meet the liturgical needs of the church. I made crucifixes, tabernacles, processional crosses, candle plates, and chalices.

Later on, Bob and I collaborated on several public commissions in Louisville and now have a bond like brothers. Because of our friendship and artistic relationship, we remember and feel the process as we explain concepts of completed collaborations to audiences. They say real men don't cry, but I guarantee that they do, and Bob and I kid about who will break down first when we give speeches or exhibits together.

Mother Mary, *bronze*
relief, St. Margaret
Mary Catholic Church,
Louisville, 1986

The Preservation Alliance Group was ready to remodel the building that we were in and we had to vacate the building. Where was I going to move? I was teaching sculpture at Jefferson Community College, where Phyllis Krantz was chair of the art department. She mentioned that a friend of hers, Ray Schuhmann, was renovating an old building that once was a Catholic girl's school, on the corner of Chestnut and Shelby Streets in the Phoenix Hill area. The site would have retail shops and he was looking for artists to be a part of it. The area was being renovated and went from drugs and prostitution to retail shops and a restaurant.

The restaurant was housed in an old church that was part of the school, and was named The Cloisters. Bernadette and I, G.C. and his wife, Sylvia Coxe, Duffy and his wife, Sherrolynn "Sherrie" Duffy, and Sammie Roland and his wife, Virginia Roland who were godparents to Kendra, were all there for the opening night of the restaurant. I remember the meal being delicious and expensive. Ray Schuhmann signed our menu.

Ray and I met and I settled into my new home. We were there for about a year and six months, but Ray's new concept for the Cloisters did not last, and we found ourselves back on the street. It was at this moment that I decided that I could not keep moving every few years. In a conversation with one of The Cloisters' tenants, Frank Longaker, a close friend, mentioned that I might want to look around the corner and see if there was anything available. Frank was a supporter of the arts in Louisville and for years he was in charge of the State Fair Art Exhibitions. Sure enough there was a wonderful building on south Shelby Street just waiting for me, but reality set in because I thought, "How in the world am I going to buy this building?" Well, God made a way and as they say, "It's all history now."

I made a decision about how to acquire my own building. When Duffy and I came across the building at 543 South Shelby Street with a "For Sale" sign on it, we broke through—well, we entered unannounced through the back plywood panel serving as a door and saw unlimited potential in the building's large space.

I didn't have a dime. Rev. Charles Tachau, Bernadette and I created and distributed an investment package. It was circulated among my art patrons in an attempt to raise enough money to purchase the building. God was on my side and several patrons invested, and the building became mine. This building was a blessing from God and I thank Him for this new studio home because I couldn't keep moving all my work from place to place.

Ed holding Kendra, Rev. Charles Tachau, and Sarah Lansdell, former art critic for The Courier-Journal, *1980 (photo by Eddie Davis)*

The year 1979 signaled a time of discovery of my own creative energies. At the same time, there was a rebirth of a group of African American artists trying to make a difference in the black community. On Sunday, June 24, 1979, a headline of the "Arts and Leisure" section of *The Courier-Journal*, written by Sarah Lansdell, art critic, read "Black artists' nerve center is vibrating; it looks like a renaissance." Indeed a great creative renaissance had begun. It was in the building at 543 South Shelby Street that all this began.

We started a group called Montage. Our goal was to be the voice for a generation of African American artists who were not getting the gallery shows their talents deserved. In the eyes of the larger art establishment, the black artist did not exist. Our mission

The Montage Group (lower l to r, counter-clockwise) Sylia Clay, Janice Carter, David Cooper, Ed Hamilton, Gretchen Bradleigh, George Tennison, William Buchanan, Andrew Jackson, Eddie Davis, Janet Finger, William Duffy, Ron Stringer, drawing is of G.C. Coxe, 1979 (photo by Eddie Davis)

was twofold: educate the general community about African American art and showcase talents.

Ken Clay, formerly Vice President of Programming at the Kentucky Center for the Arts, was an early supporter of the arts in Louisville as well as one of my patrons. He sought funding for—and provided funding—to support Montage's mission through his organization, the Renaissance Development Corp. He helped take the administrative load off of us so that we could concentrate on our work.

Black artists did exist, and we made a lot of noise. Montage was so intense that after some of our meetings at the studio, there would be several police cars outside patrolling. I guess officials thought we were plotting to overthrow the government or something. Actually, we were just meeting to talk art and figure out where our next show would be held.

From 1979 to 1980, and later again in the 1980s, I created well over twenty-seven new works for what would become my Junkology series. This series grew quite by accident. One day I happened upon a wonderful metal fragment lying in the street, and always the artist with the keen eye, I picked it up and threw it in the car. Back at the studio, it got tossed onto my ever-growing metal pile.

Out of the pile, that piece of steel was crafted into an abstract metal sculpture called *Aqua Mother.* This piece started a

Aqua Mother,
painted welded metal,
Junkology series,
owned by Kenneth
Clay, Louisville, KY,
1979 (photo by
Eddie Davis)

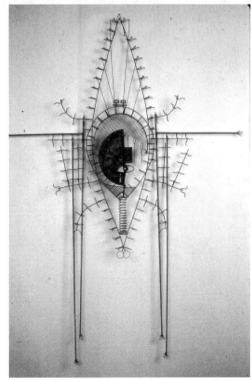

The Ju Ju Man,
welded metal,
Junkology series,
1979 (photo by
Kenneth Hayden)

Detail of Bush
Warrior, *welded
metal, Junkology
series, 1979*

*Untitled, painted,
welded metal,
Junkology series,
owned by Cecil and
Emma Talbott,
Louisville, KY, 1988*

Ed holding Kendra, Eddie, and Bernadette, opening of Junkology series at Actors Theatre of Louisville, 1980 (photo by Eddie Davis)

whole series and allowed me to use found objects of steel, tin, rock, feathers, chicken and fish bones, and other materials found in nature. Most of the sculptures I created during this period were welded and fabricated.

While rummaging through the pile one day, I became fascinated with a distinctively shaped piece of metal in the studio that was not in the pile of metal I had collected. It was an old-style ladder jack (a ladder jack is used to hold two ladders together) that G.C. had inadvertently left near my pile. I chose it to be the centerpiece of a new work entitled *Bush Warrior.* G.C. came in later and asked whether anyone had seen his ladder jack. My response was, "No, what does a ladder jack look like?"

G.C. looked around the studio, and his eyes fell upon my latest creation. He smiled and said, "Well, it looks like the main body part of your *Bush Warrior* sculpture." You can imagine how I felt at that moment, but G.C. said, "Hey, Daddy, it looks better on your sculpture than hanging off a ladder."

The Junkology show opened in the Actors Theatre first floor lobby on January 3, 1980, to great reviews. The pieces symbolized the seemingly easy discarding of objects and people.

Within a short time, a new series—the Confinement series—was born. This was an extension of Junkology, but it was based on the aspects of how man is confined by exclusion, limitations, and

Confined Man
Emerges, *mixed media,*
from the Confinement
series, 1983

frustrations. Figural elements were incorporated, such as hands
and faces, to depict the desire to break free.

My creative flow could not be stopped, and it consumed me.
Each new piece spoke to me in various ways. It was the excitement of each sculpture coming together as part of the group.
Finding new scrap metal in the streets was thrilling. There was
beauty in the patina on each piece found. I thoroughly enjoyed
composing and creating my collage-type images.

By 1983, the flow for the Junkology and Confinement series
had waned, although I did revisit the themes again later. Bronze
casting would be where I earned my reputation in the world of
art, but this period of experimentation through Junkology continued to have an impact on me. It was a time of success for me;
it was a time of high energy creating abstract compositions, and

*The first confinement
series, metal collage,
1980*

The Breakthrough,
*fabricated metal,
Confinement series,*
1985

creating artwork that was free of demands and "must look representational" projects.

I created large commissions that were realistic in appearance, but I also enjoyed fashioning sculptures that came from my creative soul and did not represent a certain person, place, or thing. It was at this point, I finally found my muse: the creation of public memorials was getting ready to break loose in the studio and would consume most of my time.

*First clay portrait of
Booker T. Washington,
1983 (photo by Eddie
Davis)*

THE BREAKTHROUGH:
THE BEGINNING OF PUBLIC SCULPTURES

THE BREAKTHROUGH: THE BEGINNING OF PUBLIC SCULPTURES

THE BOOKER T. WASHINGTON MEMORIAL

During the Christmas season of 1982, I received a visit from Kenneth Victor Young, a painter and former member of the Louisville Art Workshop. Ken was working for the Smithsonian Institute in Washington, D.C., as senior designer for the Office of Exhibits Central.

About a month after Ken's visit, I received a letter from Hampton Institute (now Hampton University) requesting a realistic rendition of Booker T. Washington for the campus. "You came highly recommended," the letter read.

I found out later that Ken was the person who gave that recommendation. He was at a conference and gave my name to Jeanne Zeidler, director of Hampton Institute's Art Museum. She was looking for a sculptor to make a representational statue of Booker T. Washington for the campus. Booker T., a famous educator, had urged his fellow African Americans to uplift themselves by using education and economic self-reliance. He was a graduate and a teacher at Hampton.

Most of my early works were either abstract in nature or liturgical pieces for churches. In order to convince the committee that I could do the sort of sculpture they required, I created a bust of Booker T. Washington, which impressed them. Bernadette had always said that my real-life representational sculptures would make me famous some day.

Prior to that, I'd never done anything on that large a scale, with the exception of working on Barney's sculptures. Even though I had the work experience, it was still difficult to believe that I was on the verge of finally achieving one of my goals, receiving a major commission out of state. I had always told Bernadette that we didn't need to move to a larger art community like New York, Los Angeles, or Chicago. I insisted that if I were good enough, I would have art projects from outside of Louisville coming to me.

I traveled to Hampton, Virginia, to meet with the committee. I had never flown before and wanted to save money, so I traveled by Greyhound bus. This was a big mistake. The bus stopped at every town and hamlet from Louisville, Kentucky, to Hampton, Virginia.

Sketch to determine scale for Booker T. Washington, *1983*

By the time I arrived in Hampton, it was almost time for me to meet with the committee and I had to rush. After I met with all parties involved and convinced them that I was the man for the job, I called Bernadette at home to tell her the good news. I also told her that I would fly home.

As the saying goes, "If you build a better mousetrap, the world will beat a path to your door." The *Booker T. Washington* commission was my proof. The contract was a one-page document, and the amount was set. I did not get to make a bid. With the knowledge I had from working with Barney, I was ready. I had everything I needed—clay, sculpting tools, my own studio space, and moral support from everyone who knew of my commission.

I conducted research on Booker T. Washington's life to get a feel for the man. Armed with that information, it was time to get to work. I planned Booker to be heroic in scale, so I arrived at a scale of nine feet. There was one small problem; I did not have sufficient height in my studio or the north light that I needed.

Looking up out of hole cut in floor to view statue at a six foot vantage point, 1983 (photo by Eddie Davis)

The solution presented itself one day when Duffy and I stood at the front door of the studio. I told him that we needed to cut the floor out of the room above and put a skylight on the roof. We went upstairs, and Duffy started to cut through the floor. Finally, as we cut out the floor and beams of a second floor room, this entire area of the studio became wide open. The light was beautiful and soft as it poured in through a window on the north wall. I knew we had done the right thing.

While working on Booker T., I was trying to establish how high the pedestal should be. I arrived at six feet, but I couldn't envision the total concept since I still did not have enough height in my studio, so the remodeling continued. I cut a hole in the floor in order to allow me to stand in the basement and look

Sketch for study of clothing, 1983

Working on nine foot full scale clay model, 1983 (photo by Keith Williams)

Booker T. Washington, *bronze, mounted on six foot granite base, 1984 (Hampton Institute photo)*

up at sculptures as I worked on them for a true height perspective. When I stood six feet down in the hole, I was at the perfect vantage point to look at Booker.

It felt good to be able to model in clay with natural light flowing over it. The clay appeared to take on a life of its own. It took about ten months of working on the clay model and another four months for the foundry to cast and finish the bronze statue.

I learned a valuable business lesson during this project. The day of the handshake for making deals is over. I was given a written estimate of $10,000 for the bronze casting. When I received the bill, however, the foundry had added another $3,000. There was nothing I could do since I had a written estimate instead of a contract. The Fine Arts Sculpture Centre, the foundry, agreed to carry the bill and let me pay it off monthly, since I had developed a relationship with the foundry personnel during the period that I delivered Barney's waxes. This lesson taught me the importance of legal advice and contracts for all parties involved. As a professional artist, I must never forget that art is a business.

A truck capable of carrying 1.5 tons was rented in Michigan to transport *Booker T. Washington* from the foundry to Hampton Institute. Duffy agreed to help me drive, but when we picked up the truck in Pontiac, Michigan, Duffy started the engine and it sounded like an ancient washing machine on its last leg. We had doubts about the truck making the trip even though we were told that we had rented the best truck on the lot.

When the foundry loaded Booker T. into the truck, a funny thing happened. All of a sudden, the truck noise smoothed out and it was as quiet as a Rolls Royce. Booker's weight helped us.

We drove all day and the next morning, while driving through Washington D.C., we were talking and not paying much attention to the exit signs. Suddenly, I did see our exit, and I shouted to Duffy, "Turn right!" That truck took that right turn on two wheels. All of a sudden, as I looked over my shoulder, Booker T. came sliding to the front of the truck. Thank God, we had him tied down. The statue could have taken Duffy, the truck, and me out on that curve.

We breathed a sigh of relief and continued on our journey to Hampton Institute. We arrived at the site, the newly designed Booker T. Washington Memorial Garden, in time to meet Dewey Wilson, the contractor charged with placing the statue on its base.

My wife, children, Mama, and Elmer Lucille Allen, a dear Louisville friend, ceramist artist, and our own personal art groupie, arrived in a rented Lincoln Towncar on the same day. The contractor and his crew took all day to put the granite facing on the support structure. As we watched and waited, I supervised the process as the statue was lifted, placed on the base, and covered with parachute cloth for the unveiling.

The next day, May 12, 1984, was the big dedication. After all the speeches were made, I started to remove the cloth. It stuck on the tip of Booker's finger, which pointed toward the Emancipation Oak Tree where Hampton slaves received the news that the Civil War was over and they were free. Finally, I gave the cloth an extra hard tug, and the statue seemed to wobble. You could hear everyone gasp because they thought Booker was going to fall off the pedestal, and I almost stopped breathing.

The architect who designed the plaza, William Milligan, came to my aid. He and I, along with Jeanne Zeidler, gave a mighty pull and the parachute cloth was removed with no problem while the statue remained in place. I did not know that the connection of the statue's feet to the pedestal was made to withstand strong wind. Therefore, Booker T. would wobble, but he would not fall down.

As we stood around talking and taking pictures, people began to leave. We realized that there was nothing else for us to do. No one had planned a luncheon, dinner, or reception to meet the artist. Dewey Wilson, the contractor, came up to us and inquired as to what our plans were for the day. He was shocked that a reception had not been planned. He took us all to dinner at a fine seafood restaurant.

Family and friends at unveiling (l to r) William Duffy, Kendra, Eddie, Bernadette, my mother, me, and Elmer Lucille Allen, May, 1984

The next day, as we left town to return to Louisville, we all crammed into the Towncar. Duffy and I were the extra passengers. While I was driving, I got so caught up in the excitement of talking about the dedication that I failed to keep within the speed limit and I received a speeding ticket.

We were sure that fame was now ours. Based on Booker T.'s importance in American history and the realistic likeness I had created, we envisioned major commissions, art selling from the studio faster than I could produce it, and worldwide newspaper coverage.

This was not the case. The dedication was mentioned in the Virginia and Washington newspapers, and *Jet Magazine,* but that was it. No replicas of the statue were requested. I was not requested to appear on *Sunday Morning* or *Today* television shows. I was just plain Ed returning home.

It was certainly lonely in my studio without the nine-foot Booker T. Life after Booker T. was depressing, so I threw myself into some studio work. I began pastel drawings with a blue motif—blue for the way that I was feeling. The work that I did during this period was in my Bluette series, which later became a show entitled "Post-Booker Blues." The Bluette concept was taken from a 1961 Dave Brubeck song that had soulfulness and moodiness to it. Bernadette gave me a Bluette party in our home.

The pain of creating something and then having to part with it is a hard process, but it is something that must happen. Little would I realize that there was something else big looming on the horizon. Get the clay ready; here we go again.

*Putting the statue's
head back on body,
1986 (photo by
Durell Hall, Jr.)*

JOE LOUIS:
THE BROWN BOMBER

JOE LOUIS: THE BROWN BOMBER

Something happened to snap me out of my funk, a letter from the Detroit City Personnel Department. The year was 1984. The letter read, "We were given your name, and we're interested in you competing to create a statue of Joe Louis." I don't know how they found me, but I'm glad they did.

When I got that letter I thought, My Lord! Here's another chance to do a biggie. Joe Louis was a great boxer and humanitarian. I sent slides of my work to Detroit as was requested. Assuming that they received the material, I waited for quite a length of time before I called them to find out if I was one of the finalists.

When I did hear from the department, I was told that city personnel had misplaced my material and slides. After finding the material, the department sent a belated and apologetic letter congratulating me on becoming a finalist.

When I do a commission on a famous person or event, I actually become a historian. It goes without saying that research on the person or event helps me to understand the historical aspects. For Joe Louis, I viewed videos of boxing matches, read his biography, and studied family and archival photographs. Luckily, Bernadette likes boxing. I had her view every tape with me, sometimes replaying and pausing the same action scene over and over. I had to memorize the visual to create the actual.

Final version of model for Joe Louis *commission, 1986*

The process of creating a working model was the next step in the national competition. Five sculptors were in the running, down from seventeen sculptors originally selected from across the nation. My model was selected, and I was awarded the commission.

In the beginning, the memorial to Joe Louis was to be life size. After I won the competition, it was announced in the local newspaper, *The Detroit Free Press*, "...a twelve-foot heroic Joe Louis has been commissioned." Well, we had to renegotiate. The first cost

Plaster model, two views, private collection, Louisville, KY, 1986

Adding clay to armature

Construction of armature to hold the clay, 1986 (photo by Keith Williams)

that I gave them did not fit a twelve-foot scale sculpture. The renegotiated contract was signed.

I began my new journey of creating the "Brown Bomber" in heroic scale. The new commission worried me because everyone in America felt they knew Joe Louis and definitely would recognize his face and his anatomy.

I felt as if the weight of the world was on me to sculpt an exact rendition. I compared the task to the way Joe Louis must have felt when he fought Max Schmeling in 1938. Joe Louis was fighting for all the people in America against the Axis Powers. I was sculpting a rendition for all the people in America.

Working high up on "Big Joe," 1986 (photo by Durell Hall, Jr.)

While working on the large-scale model, I was standing on a six-foot wooden ladder sculpting final touches on his extended right hand glove. As I was leaning in, I felt the ladder break apart. As I fell from the old, rickety ladder to the platform below, I thought this must be what it feels like to be hit by Joe Louis. I lay there for a while and checked my body for punctures from the splintered wood of the ladder. Fortunately, I was unscathed. I gathered up all the wood, looked up at Joe and said, "Damn, I need a better ladder." The next morning I had a new aluminum ladder in place.

Making the molds for casting, 1986 (photo by Durell Hall, Jr.)

The final patina being applied at foundry, 1987 (photo by Richard Hireisen)

The family at the dedication (l to r) Amy, Eddie, Bernadette, Kendra, Ed, 1987 (photo by Richard Hireisen)

Joe Louis, *bronze,*
Cobo Conference
Center, Detroit, 1987

When the statue of Joe was placed on the floor at the foundry, a person could stand between his legs and their head would not touch his crotch. *Joe Louis* is the tallest statue I've done to date.

On September 18, 1987, my sculpture of Joe Louis was put in the lobby of the Cobo Conference Center in downtown Detroit. At the unveiling, the building was unfinished, so it was raining inside the lobby because there was no roof and construction work was still on-going. The dedication committee, family members and invited guests all stood in the unfinished lobby space with our umbrellas open to keep from getting wet, dressed up in our Sunday best and with hardhats on our heads. I knew I had reached my goal when one of Joe Louis' nieces stated that it looked just like him, especially his "big feet."

It would be another three years before I would receive another commission. I kept busy doing other things, knowing deep in my heart that another commission was just down the road and waiting for me.

81

*Detail from the
African panel,* The
Amistad Memorial,
1992

THE AMISTAD MEMORIAL

THE AMISTAD MEMORIAL

Two major commissions were under my belt and my confidence level was extremely high. My wife and I took a trip to Nashville, Tennessee, to see some dear friends in the arts, Earl Hooks, Greg Ridley and his wife Gloria, and a childhood friend of ours, Dr. Larry McNeil.

Greg Ridley was a painter and sculptor of repoussé, and an art teacher at Tennessee State University. Meanwhile, I had heard that a sculpture honoring African Americans left out of history books was being planned. Luckily for me, we were visiting Earl Hooks, former chair of the Art Department at Fisk University, who had the letter of intent about this upcoming commission and shared it with me. Bernadette and I cut our visit short and got back to Louisville so that I could get my package and letter of intent to the Amistad Committee by the deadline. This potential project would be even more important than the last two larger-than-life sculptures I had created.

The commission was *The Amistad Memorial* in New Haven, Connecticut. The story behind the memorial was that Sengbe Pieh, also called Joseph Cinque, led a group of kidnapped Africans in a mutiny on *La Amistad*, a slave ship bound for Cuba. The 53 Mende Africans, led by a captured African, Sengbe Pieh, took over the ship and demanded to go back home to Sierra Leone. Because they had landed on the shores of New Haven, Connecticut, even though they were held as prisoners, they were able to earn their freedom through a court trial. If they had not, there would be no story of *La Amistad*; it would just be another episode of the many ships carrying human cargo into bondage.

I wanted to help tell the story of these proud men, women, and children fighting for and winning their legal right to freedom. The site for the statue was in front of New Haven's new addition to the renovated City Hall. I sent my package and waited for word on whether I was a finalist or not. A month went by and finally I had Bernadette call to check on the status of my submission. I was the only one who sent my material to the committee on time. So my question to them was, "Since I submitted on time then I get the job, right?" Well, not quite. I had to wait until they got more slides and curriculum vitae from other artists, and then the process would begin.

First model submitted, plaster, 1991

During the call for artists, we were instructed to submit our representation of this event. Thinking that all they were looking for was just a representation of Sengbe Pieh, we all submitted a straight standing statue. In the entries, Sengbe Pieh was either in chains, native dress, dressed in European clothing, or, in my adaptation, wearing a loincloth. I had him standing on a rock formation holding a wooden staff as if he were in his own homeland. He only had on a loincloth because I ran out of time and knew I had to meet the deadline for shipping the model to New Haven. I really didn't have time to develop him with more clothing.

All models were placed in a public bank in New Haven for the community to view. Several people from the community made the comment, …"This guy is going to get awfully cold standing out here in our New Haven weather." In the end, the committee decided that of the top five artists, three needed to come to New Haven to hear the story of *La Amistad* and the history of the Mende people of Africa. The community as well as the jury panel did not feel that any of the submitted models told the Amistad story.

Final model for The Amistad Memorial, *1992, owned by Nathaniel Green (photo by Geoffrey Carr)*

On the day of the history presentations, I was the only artist who showed up. You know what question I asked again, "Since my competitors are not here, do I get the job?" I was told "No" again; they were going to tape the session with me and send it to my competitors. While the meeting was being taped I thought to myself, wait a minute this is not fair. I requested that the camera be turned off during my explanation of how I planned to historically represent Sengbe Pieh and the Amistad incident. I certainly didn't want to give my competition a leg up. The Committee considered this a fair request, and it was honored. The competitors received a tape only about the history of the Mende people and Amistad.

It was at this point that I found out that one of the jury members had decided on another of the finalists. This often tends to happen in these competitions so you never take anything for granted and just put your best foot forward. Everything in life is political. Whoever is paying for the commission may be the only deciding factor in your winning or losing the job.

After the meeting, the finalists had a month to come back with a new concept. It was during this time that I arrived at the idea for a three-panel sculpture that told the story of the incident and honored Sengbe Pieh. How I arrived at this new concept, I'll never really know but I give credit to the history lesson I received during my committee presentation.

Sometimes ideas seem to come from out of the blue, and I am glad I thought of a solution. I was sitting at my drawing table one day trying to come up with something soon because, again, I had a deadline to meet. As I was sitting there, I started to draw the prow of a ship. Then it hit me that a bas-relief was the way to tell the story. I drew a figure within the middle of the prow concept, and everything just seemed to fall into place. Now, I not only was able to render Pieh but I could add other items on a background that related to him and the *La Amistad*. I made a 14 inch-high model, cast it in plaster, put a bronze patina on the plaster cast, and shipped it off to New Haven. In the back of my mind, I really didn't think this would fly with the jury, but it worked. I won my third important commission. Now the real work began. I had to turn the small model into the heroic scale memorial.

Working on the clay model, 1991 (photo by Clinton Bennett)

The ten-foot bronze memorial features three phases of the historical event. The first side depicts Sengbe Pieh in Africa before he and the other Africans were kidnapped. He was a rice farmer, and I depicted him with a stick in his hand. Bernadette and I were walking through Chickasaw Park one afternoon and I picked up a stick that became the stick he is actually holding. It had the length and weight in my hand that I was looking for and it is now cast in bronze. I always felt he needed something in his hand, and that he might have used the stick to hold back trees and small bushes as he walked to the rice fields.

The back panel has a scene of the courtroom trial. The third side shows Sengbe Pieh ready to board a ship back to his homeland.

The top of the Memorial is the emotional result of my research on slave trading. It depicts the body parts of Africans who were

Detail of Africans on board La Amistad

Third panel detail of Cinque holding the Bible

The courtroom panel

The Amistad
Memorial, *New
Haven, CT, 1992*

thrown or jumped overboard from slave ships. They were awash in
the vastness of an ocean; these parts represented the souls of the
many Africans who did not finish their journey through the Middle
Passage.

I was fortunate enough, under stiff competition, to have been
chosen to create the three-dimensional rendition for the entire world
to see. *The Amistad Memorial* was officially dedicated on September 18, 1992, on a day so rainy that people were soaking wet. It
was a great weekend event that will last in our memories forever.
We thought about all the rain that was falling and felt that it was
symbolic of the tears of all the Africans that did not make their
final journey home.

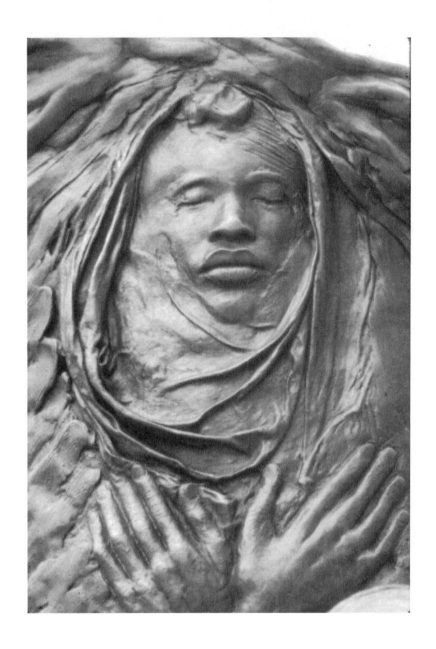

The "Spirit" from
The Spirit of
Freedom, *bronze,*
Washington, D.C.,
1998 (Richard C.
Pace Photography)

THE SPIRIT OF FREEDOM

THE SPIRIT OF FREEDOM

My three soldiers and one sailor stand with a sense of purpose, knowing battles lie ahead but prepared to fight. A family bids farewell to a departing soldier, well aware of the risks and dangers that face their loved one. Such was life for African American troops fighting in the Civil War and their families, and such is *The Spirit of Freedom.*

The Spirit of Freedom Memorial, unveiled in July, 1998, is the first to honor the participation of the colored soldiers who fought in the Union Army during the Civil War. It was an honor for me to immortalize these soldiers who, during the spring of 1865, were not allowed to march in Washington, D.C., with their white comrades-in-arms to receive the thanks of a nation. *Glory*, the movie, brought the story of the 54thMassachusetts Colored Regiment, the Civil War's valiant black troops, to life on the movie screen. *The Spirit of Freedom* keeps all colored regiments alive in bronze.

Washington, D.C., is only 600 miles and ten hours by car from Louisville, but the journey to this major commission was an entire career in the making. The statue is a testament to long hours, sleepless nights, hard work, and lots of clay that was pushed, formed, and molded to a metal frame that had to hold 2,800 pounds of weight.

I once told Bernadette that I wouldn't get this kind of assignment until I was sixty years old. I was forty-six years old when selected.

From start to finish the memorial to honor the 285,000 U.S. colored troops and their 7,000 white officers engulfed nearly six years of my life. The process began in October, 1992, when I was one of a select number of artists the District of Columbia Commission on the Arts and Humanities asked to submit work samples.

I sent my portfolio immediately and then waited for word. I dreamed of the monument. I wanted it to be molded by my fingers. Desperately, I wanted to honor the brave souls who were never given a public thank you.

Word came in December, 1992, in the form of a letter from the D.C. arts commission announcing that I was one of four finalists. I had five months to prepare, and I took advantage of the time. I did my homework, studying history books to bone up on African Americans' roles in the Civil War. I also perused articles

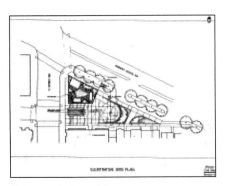

Ed's aerial view of the site at 10th and U

from the *Washington Post* sent to me by my friend, then Congressman Ron Mazzoli, to get a feel for the community and sculpture site.

The first meeting with the arts commission members, the African American Civil War Memorial Freedom Foundation, and Devrouax and Purnell Architects in association with Ed Dunson and Associates, the architectural firms designing the plaza, took place in late May, 1993, and at first everything went well. When one member made it clear to me that he preferred another artist, I thought I was dead in the water. I had my briefcase packed with stuff. My theory was they are going to ask me a million questions and I needed to be ready for anything that might happen. I brought slides because I had to show my past works and present myself to the various groups. I was dressed sharp as well and when you look your best, you feel good about yourself, and I was feeling real good.

I was the first artist to address the committee. When you go first, you set the tone. I came in armed with history and information about the neighborhood where the proposed memorial was to go. They were all shocked and wondered how I knew about what was being proposed in the U Street area. Where is he from? Kentucky? Who is this man?

I was on a roll, with only 20 minutes to present. My time ran over, and I turned to Francoise Yohalem, the art consultant who was responsible for getting the artist. I said, "Francoise I guess I should stop since my time has run out." She shook her head emphatically no. I had them captured, so I continued by saying, "Now, where was I?" I kept talking, explaining, and answering questions for another 15 to 20 minutes, while the other artists waited. When I finished, the committee members thanked me.

Before I left, there was one last question asked by Mr. Frank Smith, the gentleman responsible for this project and formerly the Ward One Representative. "Mr. Hamilton, have you ever sculpted a civil war soldier before?"

I thought a minute and stepped back. "No, I don't think I ever have, Mr. Smith. No, I haven't, but that is not a problem because that is what we do as sculptors. We solve problems." He didn't ask anymore questions. I left the room and headed back to Louisville. I felt good about that day.

Suddenly I was Mr. Businessman, flying up to Washington on the Red Eye Special, running through the airport, catching trains, catching cabs, and I loved every minute of it.

Two weeks later they narrowed the finalist down to two because the group couldn't reach a consensus. That was cool. I was ready. Bring it on. I know Washington is a city of monuments and I was ready for the battle to begin.

I spent three weeks creating a scale model of the entire memorial plaza that included my original vision of the sculpture: four soldiers and two sailors who seem to walk out of the outer side of a semi-circular wall.

When I asked Bernadette for her perspective, she pointed to the concave side of the statue and asked, "What are you going to put back here?" My response was that the other side represented the spiritual, the ethereal. This was met with my wife's all-knowing retort, "Yeah, right."

I remembered that a committee member mentioned the importance of the soldiers' families. Often the family—the mother, children, and grandparents of a departing soldier—also made the journey. I decided to add the families to the back of the memorial.

When it came time to return to Washington to meet with the two committees, I thought maybe I shouldn't take my site model. Bernadette slapped me to my senses by saying, "You better take that model with you because you may not be going back!" She didn't have to tell me twice, I packed that baby up and proceeded on to Washington.

First concept model,
clay, 1993

I presented the model to the plaza architects in July of that year, gently placing it on the floor in front of them. No details were omitted, including the scale depictions of the plaza, the monument, and subway stairs from which commuters pour; even the Masonic home across the street was included.

Within seconds, the architects got up from their seats and examined the model at eye level. They stared. They touched. They

Site model

circled. When they looked at the concave side of the statue and saw the family within, they rejoiced.

Figuratively speaking, that's when we went to church. At that point, my model was the only model of their space. It had jumped to life; even the trees cast shadows from the room lights.

In August, the committee chose my design based on the fact that I had placed attention on the entire plaza, I was a team player, and I had included a family. As I have always known, family makes all the difference in the world.

Work on the monument did not begin until the fall of 1995. It took two years to raise the funds and begin construction of the plaza at 10th and U Streets in Washington's Shaw neighborhood, named for Colonel Robert Gould Shaw, the commander of the 54thMassachusetts Colored Regiment.

Bringing "the boys," as I fondly called them, to life was a slow, meticulous process. The process started by crafting a cardboard frame for scale to determine the backdrop for the life size figures. The next few months were spent creating a metal frame from water pipes to replace the cardboard and then applying clay to the pipes. The statue stands nine feet at its highest point and curves six feet around.

Months later, the bodies of the soldiers were modeled. I narrowed the number of soldiers to three and included one sailor. I wanted it to appear as if they were walking out of the wall of clay.

*Original drawing for
the Memorial*

*Cardboard cutout to
determine scale of
Memorial*

*Spraying the "boys,"
1997 (photo by Kevin
D. Kennedy)*

Their faces, hands, and feet needed to be real enough to touch. I became obsessed with creating every crinkle around the soldiers' eyes and every crease in their pants. Viewing historical documentation I checked the authenticity of the uniforms, buttons, rifles, canteens, and shoes. In April of 1997, when representatives of the committees and members from the 54th Mass. Volunteer Regiment came to Louisville to see the final sculpture in clay before it was to be cast in bronze, they were speechless. We all breathed a sigh of relief.

The features of the family had to be real also. Bernadette's face and Kendra's hands became the models for the image of the wife left behind.

It was normal for me to spend six to seven hours each weekday and four hours on Saturdays with my "boys." They became a family for me—they became real. Since the boys couldn't speak to me in a literal sense, I played the soundtrack from *Glory* for inspiration as I worked.

Working on the older soldier, 1997 (photo by Durell Hall, Jr., The Courier-Journal)

The unveiling was delayed twice due to construction issues. My time was spent working on details, looking for things I might have missed. Then something strange began to happen. The elder soldier's face began to perspire.

The "boys" were sprayed with water and covered with plastic each evening before I went home to keep the clay moist and supple. Every morning when I returned, the bridge of the elder soldier's nose had beads of sweat. Scary, huh? It probably had something to do with an air pocket between the styrofoam and metal inside the head, but I like to think he came alive when I was not there.

I speculated that each night the boys came off the platform, played a few cards, drank a little beer, and returned to their positions before my morning arrival at the studio. Because of his age and the height of the platform and steps, it took the elder soldier more effort to get into place.

When the soldiers had been completed, I felt the area above them was too bare. With the design, the soldiers literally have

*Finished in clay, 1997
(Bill Sheets
Photography,
Louisville, KY)*

*The front side, clay
model (Bill Sheets
Photography,
Louisville, KY)*

*Children on the back
side of the monument,
clay model (Bill Sheets
Photography, Louisville,
KY)*

*A family on the back
side of the monument,
clay model (Bill Sheets
Photography, Louisville,
KY)*

Detail of sailor (Bill Sheets Photography, Louisville, KY)

Detail of soldiers (Bill Sheets Photography, Louisville, KY)

The Spirit of Freedom, *bronze, Washington, D.C., 1998 (Richard C. Pace Photography)*

their families behind them as they willingly face uncertainty for the sake of their loved ones. In times of danger on the battlefield, to whom could they turn?

Before I knew it, the face of a "protector" emerged in my mind. My former pastor, Dr. Joy Browne, came to visit during my sculpting of the memorial. We discussed the face, hands, and wing symbolism that now represent the spiritual nature of the piece. She referred me to Psalm 91:4, which reads, "He shall cover thee with his feathers, and under his wings shalt thou trust: his truth shall be thy shield and buckler." Once I read that, I knew I was right. I had to justify the face, hands, and wing symbolism on the completed model to the Commission on the Arts and Humanities because this was a change from my original design.

On Saturday, July 18, 1998, 135 years to the day the 54th Massachusetts Colored Regiment attacked Fort Wagner in South Carolina and lost 1500 soldiers in the battle, *The Spirit of Freedom* was unveiled. At the unveiling, people cried, cheered, and stood transfixed. My boys seemed truly alive amidst the thousands in the crowd. I heard it said that their eyes were looking back at those in attendance.

On the night before, July 17, the Freedom Ball, a black tie reception and gala, was held at the Hyatt Regency on Capitol Hill in honor of the unveiling of *The Spirit of Freedom* statue. The high point of the evening was the moment the Re-enactors of the 54th Massachusetts Volunteer Infantry of Company B commissioned me as an honorary captain. They presented me the captain's bars in a glass enclosed wooden frame, as Bernadette and I stood in the middle of the dance floor, looking out at family and friends. The 54th Massachusetts Volunteer Infantry of Company B stood in front of us and gave three cheers of "Hip, hip, hooray," in honor of my representation of all colored regiments that fought in the Civil War.

The next day, at 8:30 a.m., the Re-enactors' Parade was held on Georgia Avenue. The chill in the air was warmed with smiles, laughter, looks of pride, and the clicks of cameras. People were dressed in period costumes and carried flags to mark the occasion. School children, parents, grandparents, and descendants of Civil War soldiers were all represented.

The entire unveiling was broadcast on C-SPAN on that Saturday. I had had several previous interviews with Randall Pinkston, a news reporter for CBS, during the modeling, bronze casting, and installation of *The Spirit of Freedom*. The culmination of that week was a July 19th TV segment on *Sunday Morning* entitled "Of Honor and Glory."

This dedication was truly a publicity blitz. My hometown newspaper, *The Courier-Journal* sent Rochelle Riley, a Louisville reporter, to cover the events for the entire weekend. Daily, Durell Hall, Jr., a *Courier-Journal* photographer sent pictures back to Louisville to accompany the stories written by Rochelle. We visited the statue before our departure on Sunday. Even now, Louisvillians and friends who visit the site while in Washington have told us about their visits or send pictures of themselves standing beside the monument.

An elderly African American woman mentioned to me that she observed a young black man walking around the statue and looking at each figure, totally enthralled. She became concerned because he was dressed with sagging pants, the hip-hop look. She felt as though he might do harm to her or the statue. Instead, he turned to her and said, "That looks like me." I do not know what her response was, but it brought back to me the days of my youth when I lived in Louisville and saw no statues that represented the Negro population of my community.

After our arrival back in Louisville, Bernadette and I read each letter and card received from well-wishers at least twice, once silently and once aloud to one another. It was a year filled with happiness and joy. It was a year of personal understanding of how I was perceived both by people who knew and did not know me. We have learned to speak to strangers because they recognize us even though we do not know them. As Bernadette says, "Kindness is free."

For the brave men who fought for our freedom, their time has finally come.

AFRICAN AMERICAN
CIVIL WAR MEMORIAL

CHRONOLOGY OF SCULPTOR SELECTION

October 1992

Hamilton and other artists are invited by the District of Columbia Commission on the Arts and Humanities to submit materials for consideration in the commissioning of a commemorative sculpture.

December 1992

District of Columbia Commission on the Arts and Humanities informs Hamilton that he is one of four finalists.

May 1993

Hamilton becomes one of two finalists. He is invited to make a presentation to the African American Civil War Committee.

June 1993

The committee requests that both finalists prepare a design concept for their review. The artists are instructed to include the following written materials with their renderings and/or model:

1. Statement of purpose
2. Statement about the materials, dimensions, and finishes
3. A preliminary time-line to give the committee an idea of how long it would take to create the work from initial design through installation.

August 1993

The District of Columbia Commission on the Arts and Humanities informs Hamilton that he was the committee's first and unanimous choice as finalist for the competition.

December 1993

Hamilton receives confirmation from the Commission that he has been chosen for an Art in Public Places award.

LETTER FROM ED HAMILTON
(Written just before clay model was finished)

If one of my soldiers could talk, this is what I think he would say:
My Dear Father,

We know that it won't always be this way forever—this thing called slavery. I go because you can't fight any more. Your work is to stay with my loving wife and take care of our family. I know not whether I will return, but what I do know is that if I don't go, there will be no freedom for the Negro. We will be in bondage forever. One day we will own this land and our children will raise their children in freedom if God is willing.

Wife, I go to make it better for all of us. In the event I don't come back, you know I love you very much. Tell the children to be good and mind you while I am away.

Poppa and Momma, you all take care, you hear? When we return, there will be a jubilee. Well, I reckon we better get on. Bye now. We will see you all soon.

Your good son,

P.S. You tell Amy I'll make her a nicer doll when I get back. She is such a good little girl. Kiss the baby and my little man. I'll see you soon.

Complete family, back of memorial

COMMENTS FROM UNITED STATES
COLORED TROOPS RE-ENACTORS

I am ever amazed as I continue to learn of the lengths and extremes that those remarkable sable warriors of the Civil War would choose to risk in an effort to obtain freedom. I am particularly awestruck by those men who were already free and yet were willing to defy all odds, including facing the ultimate challenge of death, so that those who were enslaved would also be free.

One such unit of incredible men of color was the 54th Massachusetts Colored Regiment. The unit fought in a number of engagements, including the battle of Fort Wagner, as depicted in the movie *Glory*. Having been fortunate enough to participate in the making of *Glory* and related activities, I have come to realize just how very important and special the 54th Massachusetts truly was and is in terms of meaningful contributions to the history of this country.

This measure can easily be applied as well to the 200,000-plus men of color who made up the compliment of 139 other regiments who fought in some 440 plus engagements during those most difficult circumstances and times.

—Robert Young

During my frequent and oftentimes emotional visits to *The Spirit of Freedom*, whether I am donning the Union uniform or not, I consider it the height of honor to represent and pay homage to those exceptional regiments consisting of men of color, in particular the 54th Massachusetts Colored Regiment.

And in doing so, I stand tall, proud, and free, thanks to the courage, guts, gallantry and valor of my newfound role models, idols, and heroes: the African American soldiers.

—Mell Reid

As a Civil War re-enactor with the 54th Massachusetts, I am proud to be a part of the effort educating the public about the participation of blacks in the Civil War. I also happen to be a descendant of a Civil War soldier.

My great-great grandfather was a member of the 29th Connecticut Regiment (Colored) Infantry. Participating in battle re-enactments and living history presentations has given me a unique perspective on this subject.

Sometimes when I am in uniform in the field performing military duties, I get a strange feeling of what it really must have been like for my ancestor. I like to feel that I am reliving history in his name and hope that he would be proud of me.

—Ben Hawley

The only instantly achieved aspect of the Emancipation Proclamation implemented by President Abraham Lincoln in January, 1863, was the authorization of the use of black men, free and slave, to serve and bear arms in the War of Rebellion, as if forgetting their prior service in the Revolution against the Crown and the War of 1812. But serve they did, and they affirmed themselves as men and responsible citizens assuring the freedom of their families, their people, and themselves.

Yet this service too was diminished and forgotten, but not by all. For now we have a bronze memorial in the Capitol City depicting likenesses of the servicemen, the ones they fought to free and retrieve, and the Spirit that was with them.

The achievements of these black men in service to the Union are a great source of pride to me. It is my avocation to tell their stories and re-enact their experiences so that those who know will not forget.

—Jerry W. Brown

I never once doubted that representing the black men who accomplished so much against such daunting odds during the War of the Rebellion was a vital and proper thing to do. However, had I needed confirmation of my decision, I would have received it in the form of a casual conversation with a vacationer at the Jekyll Island Campground during our two-week stay during the filming of the Fort Wagner assault scenes for *Glory*.

A camper asked me what we were doing. When I told her that we were making a movie about the exploits of black soldiers in the Civil War, she responded, "It's fiction, right? There were no black soldiers in the Civil War, were there?"

We should set the record straight on this question, one I heard often in the ensuing years, as frequently and as accurately as possible. Our ancestors' contributions deserve so much better than anonymity. Thank goodness they now have a permanent memorial. I'm proud to have served briefly as a living memorial to their work.

—Walter B. Sanderson, II, Private,
B Company, 54th Massachusetts Volunteer Infantry

Dedication day, July 18, 1998

*Small plaster model
for competition for*
Jackie Robinson and
Pee Wee Reese
Memorial, *2001*

JACKIE ROBINSON AND PEE WEE REESE:
A DATE WITH DESTINY—9/11/01

JACKIE ROBINSON AND PEE WEE REESE:
A DATE WITH DESTINY—9/11/01

On September 10, 2001, we safely arrived in New York City by US Air. Like dignitaries, we were met at the airport by a limousine service and whisked to our hotel, Sheraton New York at 57th and 3rd. All was right with the world. I was returning to New York for an interview with the Arts Initiative Committee. I was one of five finalists for the *Jackie Robinson and Pee Wee Reese Memorial* at Keyspan Park, a minor league baseball park in Brooklyn, New York.

In July of 2001, I had my first meeting with the committee and family members of Jackie Robinson and Pee Wee Reese. The meeting took place at Windows on the World, a restaurant at the top of the World Trade Center North Tower. The concept of what the restaurant was about, and the ability to enjoy fine dining and gaze across the city and beyond was remarkable. I knew this was a place that I would revisit in the future.

When we arrived on September 10, we checked into the hotel and we had the entire day to do whatever we wanted. My meeting with the committee was scheduled for 10 a.m. on September 11. Therefore, I suggested that we have dinner at the Windows on the World. I contacted the limousine driver to pick us up and the concierge arranged the dinner time for us.

The limousine driver picked us up at 7 p.m. As we pulled up to the tower, I stood there and looked up and could not believe the scale of this building. Who would have thought that the Towers would be there one day and the next day both would be gone? Bernadette and I spent that night enjoying a meal with martinis, appetizers of lobster bisque and shrimp cocktail, a dinner consisting of sea bass and medium rare lamb with salad and vegetables, and desserts of crème bruleé and chocolate cake. We praised God, toasted life experiences, and gave thanks for blessings and lessons learned from hardships. I remember, at one point, the clouds rolled in and the entire room was closed off to the world.

The service was superb and the conversation within the room created a constant peaceful hum. Everyone was enjoying this moment in time. Later, after 9/11, we found out that others from Louisville were in the restaurant on that night. After our meal, we went to the dancing area and to look down at the Statue of Liberty. The limousine picked us up at 11 p.m. and we returned to the hotel.

When we take business trips, I usually sleep late while Bernadette is up and dressing. Women are slow dressing, or at least mine are. She watches the *Today Show* with Katie, Matt, Al, and Ann daily. Now, she suddenly called my name and told me to wake up. Something was going on. I could hear the distress in her voice. I awoke slowly and saw on the TV screen the smoke coming from the World Trade Center Building. We could hear the people describing what they saw, "I thought the plane was flying too low," and "A plane has struck the World Trade Center."

We were confused and thought it was a fire. I got out of bed and started to prepare for my appointment at 10 a.m. at City Hall, approximately three blocks from the World Trade Center. Bernadette was sitting on the side of the bed listening and watching the television intently. She said, "Ed, is that another plane or is it a television helicopter?" I responded that it was probably a helicopter. At that moment, we, and the rest of the world, discovered that it was another plane.

Bernadette was devastated. In my state of shock, I was frantic, at this point still thinking that I had to get down to City Hall for my interview.

I tried to use the telephone, but all service was gone and the cell phones did not work either. The first Tower fell and we realized that the world as we knew it had changed. By then I knew that all interviews were cancelled. The second tower fell, and we sat on the bed staring at the TV, shaking our heads and repeating, "Oh my God." We were just in disbelief.

Later, we discussed the fact that if we had not gone to dinner the night before, I would not be writing this chapter. That is because if we had been unable to go to dinner, we intended to have breakfast at the World Trade Center and then Bernadette could shop while I went for the interview. The planes struck the Towers during breakfast.

Mark Reese and his mother Dorothy (who also lives in Louisville) and several of the other artists who were to meet with the committee before me were already in City Hall during the attack and had to run for cover. Mark finally found us around 2:00 p.m. that afternoon. He came back to the hotel covered in white ash. As we ventured outside we could see the massive smoke cloud that hung heavy in the air. The ash consumed and covered everything from lower Manhattan to uptown Manhattan, as well as where the Towers fell.

Mark said that when he and the others heard that a plane hit the Tower, they didn't think much of it, not knowing what really happened. When the second plane hit, they knew it was time to get out of the building. There was a bus waiting for them, but it was land-locked and they could not get out into traffic because traffic was not moving. Then the first Tower started to fall; they turned around and headed back into City Hall only to discover someone had locked the door. They banged and banged and finally someone let them back in and took everyone to the basement for safety.

We spent the day watching the TV in our room, in the lobby, and in a ballroom in the hotel. Every word in the broadcasts was dissected and evaluated. Everyone was in a state of deep shock, shaking their heads, praying, or crying.

Police and firemen were housed in our hotel to rest between shifts. Weird events included the fact that you could order room service and receive hot food, but you could only get cold food if you ate in the restaurant in the hotel. On the first night of the catastrophe, the hotel had televisions everywhere and served a free buffet for guests. Workers trying to get into town could not get to work. Workers in town could not go home.

Every thing was at a standstill. The hotel was in a locked-down state. You had to show your room key to enter the hotel. You could walk in the streets of New York because no vehicles were allowed on the streets the next day and traffic in or out of town by train, plane, or automobile did not exist. It was surreal to say the least. We were all in a daze.

Melissa Swan and a camera crew from Louisville station WHAS-TV was in the hotel lobby on Wednesday morning, and we were glad to see them. Bernadette asked if Melissa could take us back home. She was gracious and you could see that she understood our desire to leave by any means necessary, but her van was crowded. She and her crew had driven all night to get there. Our interview with her was aired on WHAS.

Meanwhile, our children were frantic. Kendra was living in California and Eddie was in Florida and we were not able to reach them by phone until 11 p.m. that night.

We could not get out of New York. We called daily to see if our flight was scheduled to leave the airport. Finally, on Thursday of that week, Bernadette, Dorothy Reese, and I, made it to the airport but were turned back due to a bomb threat. Meanwhile, Bernadette and Dorothy ran out of medications but fortunately the Walgreens drug store and CVS Pharmacy were able to refill them. We called Mark Reese, Pee Wee's son, to tell them about our airport problems.

He contacted the hotel where we all stayed and informed them that they had made a mistake and we had not checked out. We got back to the hotel and were assigned the keys to our original room. We finally decided to wait until Sunday, the Lord's Day, and try to leave then because the airports were closed again after President Bush's arrival.

On Friday, Susanne Randolph of Susanne Randolph Art Gallery, the representative for the art commission, arranged for all of the art finalists and guests to meet for dinner at the Tavern on the Green before we left New York. "Where were you" and "What were you doing" were the topics of conversation. There was even talk of what type of art would result from the catastrophe after each artist returned home.

Saturday was spent having dinner at a restaurant with Mark, his wife Patty, and Dorothy. We all decided that we needed to get out and just spend some time together. It was not a solemn affair, but it was reflective in nature. We thought we might see a play while we were in New York and tried to get tickets to see the *Lion King* but the price remained $165 though the city was closed and the theater seats were mostly empty. I told Bernadette she could wait until the show came to Louisville. I was not paying $165 for her to see some puppets. Considering the circumstances, I don't really think we would have enjoyed it had we seen it.

Bernadette and I now understand the meaning of "It's not your time." We were close to the Towers, only five or six miles from the area. We could smell the damage of the fire in the air. The constant smoke that continued once the flames were extinguished was highly distressing to Bernadette. The white ash that floated and settled over the city was as fine as baby powder.

We probably needed some sort of psychiatric help. We cried off and on for a year after we got home. We had to stop watching the news channels and reading articles about 9/11 in order to heal. We have always understood and appreciated our blessing, and we still pray for those who lost loved ones and for the brave police and firemen who risked their lives.

I always believed that God puts you where you are needed. I wanted to be the one to sculpt these two great men who changed the direction of major league baseball, but it was not to be. It turned out that someone else ultimately won the job, but as the door closed on this commission of Jackie and Pee Wee, another giant of history, York, the slave of William Clark, would consume my time for the next three years. I was chosen to sculpt York, an unknown slave, who would take his rightful place in history along with the others whose memorials were created by my hands.

Finished clay of York,
2003

THE YORK MEMORIAL

THE YORK MEMORIAL

Louisville was one of 15 official sites of a national commemoration celebrating the bicentennial anniversary of the expedition of Meriwether Lewis and William Clark. Louisville was where the two explorers met before embarking on their historic mission to explore the West. York, Clark's slave, was an unofficial team member of the Corps of Discovery. How did I get involved with and become interested in the York experience?

James Holmberg, curator of special collections at the Filson Historical Society in Louisville, pushed for the bicentennial commission to include Louisville in its plans. He is extremely knowledgeable about the Lewis and Clark expedition and had written an epilogue to the book *In Search of York* by Robert Betts. Jim thought it would be fitting to honor York with a monument, and he and the Louisville Area Bicentennial Committee approached me about doing a heroic-size bronze of York.

From its beginning, I have been honored to be a part of the project. Jim and I were in the East Room of the White House on January 17, 2001, when President Bill Clinton made York an honorary sergeant for his work with Lewis and Clark. The event was Clinton's last in the East Room before he left office on January 20, 2001.

The York Memorial was to be a lasting legacy for Louisville when the bicentennial celebration arrived in Kentucky in the fall of 2003.

The memorial was commissioned by the City of Louisville under the leadership of Mayor David L. Armstrong. *York* stands on the Belvedere, a prominent downtown plaza, gazing toward the Falls of the Ohio River, where Lewis, Clark, and the Corps of Discovery members assembled before their departure for St. Louis in October, 1803.

I accepted the task of creating a comprehensible York because I considered this statue to be a source of historical instruction and a civic icon. I hoped the statue would play an influential role in shaping our sense of York whose experiences as a black American in the early nineteenth century were, without exaggeration, unique and truly extraordinary.

First concept sketch of York

Even before I had any sketches on paper, I did research on York. I remember asking myself, "Who was this man?" In the beginning, I read Robert Betts' book, *In Search of York*, and Stephen Ambrose's *Undaunted Courage*, as well as letters written by William Clark, journals kept by members of the Corps, and anything else I could get my hands on. We can assume York was illiterate, as there was nothing written in his own hand. It is hard to know because, as a house slave, he might have had opportunities to gain knowledge of reading while performing duties for his young master, William Clark.

I had to get into the history and feel some of the things that York might have felt. I studied pictures of slaves, especially those with more prominent African features, since York may have been only three generations removed from his African ancestors. I studied the clothing and weaponry of the day. I interviewed Holmberg and other historians for relevant information.

During my research, I gleaned a lot of information about York. He was never an official member of the Lewis and Clark expedition party. He was a master hunter, knew how to handle firearms, and how to track and survive in the woods, yet, he was simply known as Captain Clark's slave.

York proved to be indispensable to the Corps of Discovery when the group encountered the Arikara Indians. They had never seen a black man before and believed him to be spiritually powerful. They named him "Big Medicine" and he became a diplomatic tool for Lewis and Clark with the Native American Indians throughout their three-year journey to the Pacific Ocean and back. I wanted to see York as the Native Americans did. They accepted him for his ability and strength, not as a slave to white explorers.

Congress had authorized the Corps of Discovery to travel from the Mississippi Valley to the Pacific Coast in order to chart unknown territories and find a viable commercial route across the continent. In mid-November, 1805, after months of dangerous exploration, York and the Corps of Discovery members finally reached the Pacific Ocean. York was the first African American, enslaved or free, to cross the United States from coast to coast. When he returned to Washington in 1806 after achieving the mission set by President Thomas Jefferson, he was not recognized as an American hero. He did not meet the President—York had to wait outside.

Once the celebrations died down, York returned to a life as Clark's slave. He wanted his freedom, and made numerous requests and pleas to Clark, but was not freed until ten years later. Clark wrote about this in letters to his brother, Jonathan, complaining of York's stubbornness about wanting to be set free.

I took York's story to heart and was energized by trying to put a face to the man. I knew that what I put in his eyes would tell the story of what he went through. Although there are no known drawings of York, as a black person and a by-product of slavery, I tried to understand the world through his eyes so that I could create his face. My goal was to give both a face and a voice to someone forgotten, someone who was almost lost to history forever.

After conducting months of research on York, I had to figure out how I would represent his persona. My creative juices started to kick in. I started drawing and making small clay models to figure out what direction I would take. How would I put this particular person in his own place in time? How would I capture such a man with his character and great strength in a statue?

My whole outlook was to put him in his own time and space and to get away from some of the stereotypical or negatively written information that was so prevalent in that era, that of the loyal slave, the buffoon, and/or the "happy servant." The only written description of York was that he was as "big and black as a bear." This is what Clark wrote about him in his journal.

I wanted to create a piece that would be heroic and reflect great strength. I wanted to create a monument that a person could stand next to and not be afraid of just because he was a large figure of a black man, so I focused on capturing a sense of the man.

How could I portray York as a human being? Although he was under the shackles of slavery, he had to feel triumph in being part of a historic expedition. I let my mind deal with York in terms of freedom versus slavery. In my mind, I put a face on him, a face of strength but lined with cares. I didn't want him to look pained, but I didn't want him to be perceived as a "happy" slave. I started the process of creating York's image by sketching with pen and pencil then later making pastel drawings. Once I felt good about them, it was time to start work on the clay model.

I created a 13 inch clay nude model and a clothed one as a frontiersman with a large, felt floppy hat and full, cotton shirt. I was still trying to get the feeling for York as a person. I sent the small-scale nude model version to CyberX-3D, a digital enlargement company based in California. They shipped an eight-foot styrofoam model back to me in two pieces, a torso from the waist up and a lower torso, down to his feet. York came back with no arms because the small-scale version was armless.

Eight foot styrofoam model as clay was added, 2002

I normally make an iron armature structure bolted to a base, then take pieces of styrofoam and add to it and carve it down so that I don't exceed the area of where the skin is to be. The styrofoam model simplified the putting of clay on a metal frame, so I did not have to weld a metal framework armature.

Now it was a matter of putting two four-foot sections together to complete an eight foot tall figure. I really just needed a blueprint of the body portion to create large-scale arms that would be moveable. I could make adjustments, if needed, as I moved further along in the process. Once I got the figure filed down, removed visible seams and shaped it the way I thought it should be, I shellacked the whole foam figure. Satisfied with the form, I knew it was time to start the clay process.

I literally started slapping wet clay on the styrofoam body. I used my fingers and large tools I have created throughout my years of sculpting to start giving shape to York. I usually make the body first. Once I get that right, and everything feels right, its only then that I start to model the clothes. When viewers see the piece with the clothes on, they should feel that there is a breathing body underneath the shirt and pants, and that there are feet in the shoes.

My main thought, as I first put the clay on, was to get the figure correct and the form to work. At this point York was not yet a person. He was a form with a layer of clay just before he took on a personality. I wanted to see how light flowed over his body. Once I felt that I had seen his figure in the light and how the light bathed him, I turned him and looked at him from all sides.

Next, I got into the detail work and pulled out the personality of his face. How did I want to portray him? Should he look directly at the viewer, or look into space? I tried to put myself into his thoughts as he looked out over the horizon at God's creations, seeing things he had never seen before and might never see again. For that brief moment, what was he thinking? That's what I tried to put into his gaze.

I really got into the personality. He became alive to me. What I wanted was the moment when the figure said to me, "Yeah, I'm here, now leave me the hell alone." Was it important to show every single vein and crease and wrinkle? I didn't believe it was. I was more interested in seeing how a statue looked at the viewer, a certain tilt of the head and the creases in the brow. I wanted to go just far enough to capture the personality and no further. Personality is in the hands and eyes, and everything develops around them.

As I looked at *York* standing there, partially in the buff, the whole concept of "Big Medicine" hit me. Did I capture what the Native Americans saw in him? They did not see a slave. They saw a powerful black man who was so unlike all the white men with him that he deserved a new name, "Big Medicine." They saw a tall man, a man with a viable presence, and a man with strength and ability equal to theirs.

It seemed to me, at the time, that if I put a hat and sleeves on *York,* he could be any black man standing up on a pedestal. I wanted to strip him down, get those sleeves off the shirt, take off the hat, and let the viewer deal with the brow, with the head, with the gaze, with those arms holding a rifle and the ducks he had shot. I wanted the viewer to see the veins and imagine blood pulsating through his arms in order for *York* to appear as a real person standing before them.

During the process of creating a sculpture, I videotape my work. Doing so allows me to see things that I couldn't see up close and personal. It is also good for me to document the process of creating a sculpture. This I did with *York*.

Once the clay figure was finished and approved by the *York* Committee and Mayor Armstrong, it was a matter of preparing the clay figure for the bronze casting. This is the part of the process where the artist has to let the sculpture go. This is the death of the clay but it is also a resurrection—the rebirth of the clay to bronze.

Foundry technicians, working from The Bright Foundry of Louisville, came to my studio and painted rubber mold material all over the entire piece. They put plaster molds on top of the rubber. When the rubber was cured and became solid, they took the plaster molds off, cut the seams where the rubber was and laid each section of rubber back into the plaster molds. This was necessary in order for the rubber to maintain its shape.

Then they took the pre-numbered sections of the plaster and rubber molds off the clay model and delivered them to the foundry. The numbers assisted the foundry employees with placing all the sections in the correct order before welding.

The next step, performed at the foundry, was to take hot wax and paint it into the negative surface of the rubber molds. These molds had picked up the actual impression of the surface of the original clay model. The clay is positive; the molds become their negative. When the wax cooled, the rubber was pulled off of the wax patterns. I inspected all the waxes to make sure every nuance that I crafted in clay was detailed in the wax.

These sections were taken into the slurry room. Slurry is a ceramic shell material the thickness of pancake batter. Foundry employees dipped the wax patterns down in the slurry, pulled them out, took them to the sand vat, and sprinkled fine sand over the wax patterns. The ceramic shell solidified on the wax surfaces in an even coat. The process was repeated several times to get the proper thickness of slurry.

When the waxes were ready to be burned out of the ceramic shell molds, they were taken to the burnout furnace in another building of the foundry. The molds were all stacked upside down in the furnace so that the wax ran out, hence the name "lost wax process." After the wax was melted from the molds, they appeared pure, clean, and white inside, which meant that all the carbon had burned out and that no residue wax was left in the molds.

While the burnout furnace was burning the wax out of the molds, the crucible was waiting to receive the bronze ingots, solid bars of bronze similar in shape to gold bars. Air and gas would be mixed together to melt the bronze ingots in the crucible to the right temperature of 1900 to 2000 degrees when the ingots became liquid metal.

The heated ceramic shell molds were placed in the sandpit. The employees picked up the crucible full of hot melted bronze ingots and poured the bronze into the molds. The melted bronze poured like water down into the molds. You could hear the sound of the molds filling with the melted bronze. Once the ceramic molds were filled to the top, the process was complete.

About a half-hour later, a craft person took a hammer and broke the mold material off. Bronze sections of the sculpture came out exactly like the wax images. Finally, *York's* bronze sections were welded together.

*Detail of head of
York,* 2003 *(photo by
Geoffrey Carr,
Louisville, KY)*

Detail of York's *left
hand holding a rifle*

The next step in the process was to create a suitable base for *York* to be placed on. I didn't want my *York* to be placed on a traditional pedestal. Statues on pedestals usually end up standing on a square marble or granite base with names of contributors, contractors, the sculptor, and others engraved on it.

I had envisioned, in the early concept stage, that York would be standing on a rock bluff, looking toward the vast plains and the mountain ranges as the Corps of Discovery journeyed toward the Pacific Ocean. I wanted to see York looking into the wind, the spray of water upon his brow and in his own time and space. I wanted his strong gaze looking toward the river, coming home, as a fulfilled person experiencing what a slave normally would not have been allowed to do.

In order to do this, I contracted with Forest Boone, president of Museumrock Products, a company based in Louisville. Through our collaboration, he brought York's rock bluff into reality. York now stands on a man-made 22,000-pound sculpted rock formation overlooking the Ohio River. It is all that I expected and more.

Sometimes I look at him and his expression says, "My Lord, look at all this vastness. Look at where we are going and what we're about to do." In my heart, I know that he could see it, the sheer greatness of a tremendous human endeavor. Maybe he

The finished bronze statue standing on the rock formation, 2003 (photo by Geoffrey Carr, Louisville, KY)

thought, "My God, now I have to go back to Kentuck', back into bondage, to serve my massa once again after all I have done. Lord, have mercy!"

The time had arrived for York to take his rightful place in history. On October 14, 2003, a stormy and rainy day, the *York* Committee, Mayor Jerry Abramson, former Mayor David Armstrong, and I unveiled *York*. The weather appeared to be an exact duplicate of the departure day of the Corps of Discovery on October 14, 1803. Since Louisville was a major part of the Lewis and Clark Bicentennial Celebration there was national and local media coverage of the unveiling. A large number of people including family, friends, my personal art groupies, community and state dignitaries, people from across the Ohio River from southern Indiana, and school children were there to witness the momentous event. It was an event that I shall never forget. It was

Dedication Day, with the York *Committee and Friends, including Mayor Jerry Abramson and former Mayor David L. Armstrong, Oct. 14, 2003*

a proud moment to bring York to life on the very riverbanks where he traveled some two hundred years ago. This man who only wanted to be free, as he had been for three long years, now stands eight feet tall and free for all eternity. Truth is, if York were alive today and standing on this spot looking at my sculpture, I think I know just what he would say, "Thank you, Lord. At last, somebody's told my story."

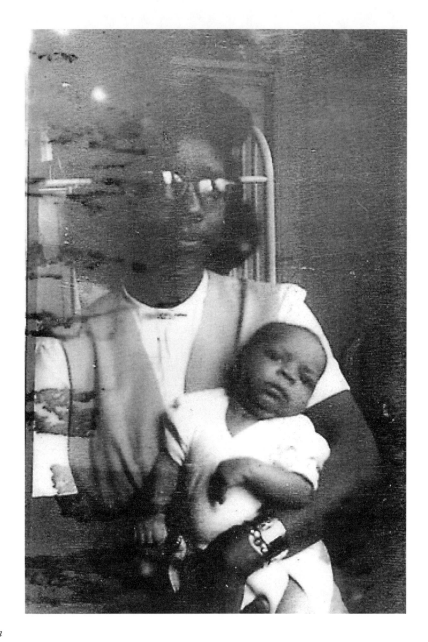

Virginia and Marvin
Revere

EPILOGUE
SECRETS: THE DISCOVERY OF A LIFETIME

EPILOGUE
SECRETS: THE DISCOVERY OF A LIFETIME

Secret, the word Webster's Dictionary defines as 1) kept from, or acting without, the knowledge of others, 2) beyond general understanding; mysterious, or 3) concealed from sight; hidden.

My artistic life began in grade school. My professional life began after college. My book writing began in 1998. My quest for truth began in November, 2002. All these experiences have helped me believe in the old saying, "Nothing happens before its time. . . birth, life experiences, or death."

Ever wonder how you would feel if the people in all the family pictures that you looked at over and over for decades were not the people you thought they were? That those who tended all your needs, who fed you, who clothed you, who cared for you through sicknesses, were not who they said they were?

You were told all your life that you look just like your daddy or your mama. What about your extended family such as your aunts, uncles, cousins, nephews, and nieces? Would it make any difference to you once your true origins had been revealed to you? Should some truths be left untold and taken to the grave?

My response would be I don't think you just throw away fifty-seven years of your life because you now know that the blood in your veins is not the same as theirs. The real blessing in this story is that a baby was born, loved, and left for two and a half years in an orphanage unknowingly waiting to be adopted. Finally, this baby was selected by two people and brought to Kentucky and raised as their own. I have lived this story and its effects on me have, at times, been overwhelming.

I recall that after I learned my real story, I had to go to my pastor, Rev. Charles Tachau, and share my story and my feelings with him. His words guided my heart to accept all things that happen in life, good or bad, and to be open to the blessings that I had and will receive. Many things happen to us for a reason, and we don't always have the answer for everything. Yet, what an incredible life I have experienced.

This is the story of my journey to find my birth mother, and my hope that she was alive and well and wanted to see me. Maybe the final chapter of *A Journey of Discovery*, my adoption story, will give hope to those who might have someone they may be searching for, a parent or loved one. They may be out there just waiting for someone to make a connection. Ultimately, my birth mother gave me her reason for not searching for me, but I began to wonder why my brothers or sisters did not search on her behalf. I discovered that my sister Paula wanted to start the search but my birth mother thought it would mess up my life and stopped family members from beginning the quest. She told them, "He will find me." I did. She is a Christian woman and her faith that everything will turn out right through prayer served her well.

People say that some things are best left buried with the dead, and people of my mom's generation were well equipped to carry certain secrets to their graves. Unfortunately for me, all of my close relatives, such as my aunts and uncles who could have shed light on a mystery that haunted me for as long as I can remember, never shared their knowledge with me. I can imagine that Mama swore them to secrecy.

The innuendoes about my adoption became more frequent when I became an adult. As a child I always felt that there was a window that I just could not close all the way, nor could I find anyone to open it wider. It seemed to me that the window was always cracked, raised an inch or so, just enough to let a small breeze in and make the curtains flutter but not enough to let in the words and answers I needed to hear. The secret was always there, surrounding me and trying to choke my spirit. It was evident in some comments and the way Mama reacted to certain situations. Call it a sixth sense. It was something that I just felt but had no way to explain.

The rumors were started by friends of the family and later by family members. As a married adult, I always had people who remembered me as a child playing in our family's tailoring, dry cleaning, barber, and shoeshine shop. Because I still live in the close-knit African American community of Louisville, I am always approached by people with whom I went to school or church, or people who knew me as a child, even people I don't know who want to wish me well. Often the conversations start out with a friendly hello, then move to community or art issues and then out of the blue, a comment will be made, "You know she's not your mama, or you know he's not your father."

My expression and response was always confusion, which would cause them to immediately change the subject. When these comments came from people I respected and had known for years, I was shocked. I wondered what their motive was, or even if they had one. They were in their late sixties or older, so why say this now? Was this something they wanted to share before they passed on to glory, was it vindictiveness, did they believe that my mama and daddy were not good enough to have a talented child, or were they jealous? The answer is they thought I knew the truth and probably were waiting for me to name my real mother and father.

I have discussed these events and feelings with my wife, Bernadette. Early in our marriage, she told me that her grandmother, Anna Bishop, had shared with her before we married that my mama was not my real mother. She never explained who my father was to Bernadette. I was OK with this information because by then I had been dealing with the rumors for several years.

I want you to understand that the subject of my birth did not come up on a daily basis, but it did raise its head enough to be needed to be resolved. Bernadette and I would take out family pictures and look hard for resemblances or differences—I had my mama's eyebrows or my daddy's chin. We even made up our own conclusions. My daddy was 23 years older than Mama was when they married; therefore, in scenario one, maybe she was already pregnant. In scenario two, my mama couldn't have children and I was the product of my father's rumored love affair with a white woman in Cincinnati, or in scenario three, my mama couldn't have children and I was the child of a family member who became pregnant and didn't marry. In some families, unmarried family members have given children to favorite aunts or other family members to avoid adoption by strangers or instead of abortion.

Of course, I could not get Mama to even talk about it. Her defenses went up and the conversation was closed. In a sense, I guess I started to wonder why even bother. I had lived past childhood, been raised well, and created a life of my own. I raised two children, Edward III and Kendra, and have a great wife.

Still, I just wanted to find out and put the rumors and lies to rest because that's all they were to me until I found out the truth.

My need to know who I am, and where I come from was too great of a challenge for me to not explore. It all began when I started writing the first draft of this book, then entitled *The Birth of a Monument*. It was only after disclosure of my adoption and the discovery of my birth mother that the title was changed to *The Birth of an Artist: A Journey of Discovery*.

I needed information on the jobs of my father and other family history for the book. Juanita White, a friend, writer, and educator, along with her cousin, LaVerne Shumake Dunning, started the process of investigating my family history, beginning in Bardstown, Kentucky. Since I had been told all my life that my father's family came from Bardstown, this was the logical starting point. A lot of the information found was taken from early census records, death certificates, and birth records. As we started the search, we were trying to connect a Union soldier from the Civil War to my daddy's side of the family. Inconsistencies surfaced when I found information on my dad's and mama's family, but could not find any connections for me. In fact, I could not find my birth register.

All my life I wondered why I was born in Hamilton County, Ohio. I always tried to rationalize that my parents were passing through Ohio, and Mama could not get back to Louisville in time for my birth, so she had me there. I thought this was a good answer and it could have happened. Never once did any of the family lead me to believe anything else. In my child's mind this made sense, so when anyone asked me why I was born in Cincinnati, that was the story I nonchalantly told.

After years of hearing the rumors and wondering, the mystery finally revealed itself on a warm afternoon in the winter of 2002. Mama had taken ill. She was 94 years old, suffering with a little dementia and low blood sugar attacks from her poor dietary habits. I had gone to the store for her and when I got back to the house, I found her passed out on the floor. I quickly dialed 911 and they sent an ambulance. I realized right then that Mama could no longer take care of herself and something had to be done.

Prior to this, over 18 months, we had tried to keep her in her house with the help of my cousin, Barbara Dawson, who continues to be a big help to me with my mother. At first, Bernadette and I delivered my mother cooked meals that she could heat in the microwave. We had relatives and friends sit with her during the day for company, and put her on the church van pick up list, because she was still active in her church.

When the medical team arrived, they stabilized her and proceeded to take her to the hospital. Everything was in disarray as she fought hard not to leave her house. Sometimes I felt she loved that house more than Daddy or me. She was 94 years old, yet fighting the medical team tooth and nail. I think they were just as shocked as I was at the battle she put up to stay.

Once they left with her, I looked for her purse and any medication that I needed to take with me to the hospital. As I was searching for these items, I noticed that Mama's mattress was in disarray and half off the bed. When I started to put it back in place, I noticed a lump underneath it. Reaching under the mattress, I pulled out a small purse, but thought nothing of it until the next day.

During the exam at the hospital, the doctor noticed a scar on Mama's abdomen and questioned her as to its cause—had she had a baby or a hysterectomy? She told the doctor that she had not had a baby and I was adopted. The doctor questioned me about her statement because my mom exhibited evidence of dementia. I informed the doctor that she had not told me that I was adopted. I was stunned at being questioned. Why would she tell this information to a stranger and not to me? Her secret was inching closer to the surface of my life.

After leaving the hospital, I returned to the house and started going through several purses. Then, I opened the purse that had rested under the mattress. I didn't know how long or why the purse was there. Mama believed in banks so I knew there would not be money in it.

What it did contain was a secret treasure, but of a different kind. I found some old papers that were now yellowed after being hidden and folded many times. I opened them carefully, as they were ready to fall apart. I could not believe what I was actually staring at. Here were the papers that offered up the truth after all these years.

They were the original adoption papers. I had thought they existed and they did. Now, I knew why Mama stayed in the bed so much, like a mother hen nesting on her egg, protecting her secret all these years. These papers sent me into an emotional tailspin for quite sometime. Now all the rumors could be laid to rest.

I have asked myself over and over why she held on to these papers. She was never going to tell me about the adoption, and if she had not kept them, I would never have known how to go about finding my birth mother. I thank God she did save them for whatever purpose she had in mind.

Later, my wife, children, and I would shake our heads and speculate on why she kept the documents. Finding them shed light on some of Mama's behavior, but we would have had to talk to her to get a true understanding of her motivation and we knew that was not going to happen.

Armed with the adoption papers, my new journey started in February, 2003, at the Family Court building on Eighth and Jefferson Streets in downtown Louisville. I arrived with the yellowed documents in hand; I stepped up to the counter and handed one of the sheets to the receptionist and requested copies of my birth and adoption records. The clerk recognized me as Ed Hamilton, the sculptor. What was strange to me at the time was that the clerk was named Norton, which was my middle name. I thought that this was surreal, since what are the odds on running into another person with Norton in their name?

We chatted for a moment because she was a performance artist who wanted to be a professional artist on her own some day. We finally got around to the reason why I was there and I discovered the process wasn't as easy as I thought it would be. The records are closed files and only by a valid and special request can you even think about seeing them.

I started filling out the papers she handed me, realizing I had to have two good reasons for my request of information about my birth records. I wrote that I needed to know what my health issues were now that I knew I was not the natural born son of the mother who raised me. Second, I stated that I would like to close this chapter of my life by knowing the truth of my adoption. We had always assumed that I would live into my 90s or longer, like my mama's side of the family. Now what was my life expectancy, and what illnesses could I expect as I aged?

I finished filling out the application and handed it to the clerk. She told me it could take six months to a year to receive a response back. I replied, "I have waited this long, what's one more year."

I left the courthouse and I waited and waited. Finally, after six months I called the court only to be told that something was coming, but not yet. This waiting and anticipating was upsetting me. My fear was that the whole process could stop if my birth mother did not want to see me, and that scared me. I wanted to know her, to see her, and just to know that she was still alive and well. I tried not to dwell on the possibility that she might be dead.

At the beginning of the process of my request for my birth mother's information, Mama had to enter a nursing home. Committing her broke my heart because she was a woman of independence and self-reliance.

I remember my childhood friends nicknamed her the "Red Baron," because she used to ride around in her black Corvair with a shiny black cap on her head and a white scarf around her neck, which would blow in the wind.

She has always been strong-willed, often to a fault. She knew what she wanted and wasn't afraid to go and get it, and had made the decision to be a barber, not a beautician, in the 1940s. She saved money from the business to build a new three bedroom stone house on a hill in the west end of Louisville in 1958. She cared for me and worked in the business daily with my daddy while maintaining her church and social activities.

Mama raised me with encouragement and strictness. It was a challenge then and now for a single female parent to raise children alone. I wasn't disrespectful or highly disobedient, but I wanted to play and go out and be with my friends. I didn't like being challenged and questioned about what was asked and what I said whenever I returned home from visiting with family and friends.

I realize now that her anxiety was due to her secret. I loved her and wanted her love in return but I never understood that the secret was the reason for her behavior and mood swings. I truly believe that the secret kept her from relaxing and giving her full self to others and me. The fear of rejection is strong in all humans. If she had told me after the death of my father, she probably felt I would have used the adoption against her anytime that she disagreed with what I wanted to do, or when I felt she was being mean or unfair. This is what children do.

I remember her being quite loving when I was a small child, but I couldn't move out of her shadow, and heaven forbid if she didn't know where I was at any given time of the day. I recall that when I would get on my bike, I would leave the apartment for hours on end, the wind smacking me in the face, as I peddled away. What a sense of freedom I had with my bike.

I was coming of age, and it was just Mama and me. I think she became anxious that I might start asking questions about my birth and that is why she attempted to control my comings and goings. She was suspicious of my friends and anyone that she did not know. Like most people who hide something, she could never be sure that someone she had confided in had not told someone else. She did not want to have to tell me about the secret that she had kept all those years and she wore her silence like a cloak of armor.

There was one major thing that Mama did do for me. Though she did not always understand my art, she supported all my efforts in becoming the artist and sculptor that I am today, often telling me that I could do anything, which I heard so often that I began to believe it.

For six months I waited, hoping that my file was received. It was another four months—a total of ten months—before I received word. When I finally got the call, it was all I could do to get down to Family Court fast enough. All the while I was wondering what I would find out and did I really want to know? I had come this far and the records were there, so it was too late to turn back.

I arrived at the courthouse, took a number and waited. When I heard my name, my knees were trembling as I made my way to the counter. I stood there with trepidation, my hands sweating, afraid of what I was going to find.

The lady behind the counter escorted me to a back table and handed me a long, fat, yellow faded folder, saying, "Take your time." I must have sat there for ten to fifteen minutes before I said to myself, "Ed, open up the folder, you have come too far to turn back now." Wasting no more time, I opened it and my whole life changed forever. It was all there—where I was born and the names of my birth mother and my grandmother. In a flash, all the lies that surrounded my birth were dispelled and cast out.

I was born on February 14, 1947, in the Catherine Booth Home in Cincinnati, Ohio. This facility was run by the Salvation Army as a residence for pregnant teens. My birth name was Marvin Revere and my birth mother's name was Virginia Revere.

The tears welled up in my eyes and I thought about how hard it was to find out this information so late in life. Why did my parents' generation keep so many secrets, and why, even more importantly, was I given away? My head was spinning and yet, somehow, I kept saying to myself "Thank God, Thank God." At last the truth was revealed.

Now, as an adult I just wanted Mama to talk about her side of the story, but her increasing dementia made this impossible. I think it is probably better that my adoption revelation happened when I was an adult with a family of my own than when I was a teenager without a father's support.

Before he died, my daddy and I had a true male bonding, and I knew I was the apple of his eye. He was always there for me, even though he was constantly working. I would sit on his lap and he would give me coffee or whatever I would ask for even when Mama objected. I would sit on the big counter in his tailoring and cleaning shop and watch him work. He made wool suits for me that itched. His hands had grace as he cut fabric for suits, and wrote letters and notes for the bet booking operation he ran on the side. I could come in the bedroom and jump up and down on his bed. He would laugh and never object.

How strange it all seems to me that I had been searching for family history on the Hamilton side. I now realized that I had been searching in all the wrong places to find out who I really am. People who came up to me in the past and stated, "My family is from Bardstown, Kentucky. I think we are kin," weren't really linked to me at all. Some even started genealogical searches about my family. I would acknowledge their research, but even then I didn't put any faith in them. Again, in my opinion, early revelation of the secret could have caused a schism between Mama and me. I know now that God knew what He was doing by giving me knowledge of my adoption when I could handle it better as an adult.

The adoption was official on Friday, September 2, 1950, and I was brought to Louisville by my adopted parents, Edward Norton Hamilton, Sr. and Amy Jane Camp Hamilton. There was a section in the file that struck me. It was Section Five entitled "Adjustment of Child and Petitioners to Each Other." It stated, "We feel that the adoptive candidate has made a good adjustment since his placement in this home. He was quite withdrawn at first, but has become more sociable and outgoing. He appears happy and well-cared for and adoptive parents give every indication of being devoted to this child."

You see this was not the end but a new beginning for me with Daddy and Mama, a love affair of two people who worked hard to make a home and to be a complete family in spite of this well-kept secret. I shall always be grateful for their love and sacrifice, yet the truth does rise to the top. I found myself wanting to search and find out who I really am. The question that troubled me was, "Do I really want to know who and where my birth mother is and if she is still alive?" I thought a moment, and my answer to that was one word, YES, unequivocally YES, without question, YES. The search was on and indeed I wanted to know.

I had the papers, but the information on them really wasn't telling me anything. Of course, there was quite a lot of legal jargon, but I didn't see anything that would allow me to find my birth mother. At this point, I contacted my friend, Juanita White, who had helped me search for information about the Hamilton side of my family. I asked Juanita what direction we should take. She stated that we needed to request a death certificate for my grandmother and a birth certificate for my birth mother. I sent forty-five dollars to the Office of Vital Statistics in Cincinnati, Ohio, in my birth name of Marvin Revere.

It took several months for the certificates to come in the mail. When they arrived, I looked and looked for some connection to my birth mother but I just couldn't put it together. The main reason was the "Information Relative to Filing a Delayed Birth Certificate." Children put up for adoptions are not issued a birth certificate until they are adopted.

My birth mother's vital information was right there all along but I couldn't see it. I called Juanita and we went over the death certificate of my grandmother, Emma Revere, line by line. She finally asked me, "Whose name was on the informant line?"

I said, "Virginia Rakestraw," and there was a pause before Juanita spoke.

She said, "That's your birth mother."

You could have knocked me over with a brick.

Then Juanita said, "I'll call you back."

When she called back, she said, "I found your birth mother. She was listed in the phone book of Dayton, Ohio, and her phone number is ———."

"Oh my God," I shouted.

"Are you going to call her?" Juanita asked

I replied, "Well, I am not sure, but I guess I will." Juanita said she would call me back in a half-hour, and I said, "Ok."

Half-hour went by really quickly and, yet I could not make my fingers hit that phone number. I just couldn't do it. Juanita called me as promised and asked if I had called and I said, "No." There was a short pause over the phone line.

Then she said, "Do you want me to call for you?"

I said, "Juanita, yes I do. Please, you know how to deal with these issues and you have a way of asking the right questions. I wouldn't know what to say."

She said, all right, and that she would pray on it and call me back. Right about then my nerves were on edge and my heart was pounding a mile a minute. I had no concept of what she would call back and say. If Juanita spoke with my mother, would she be receptive, would she want to speak with me; what would I say to her, "Hi, am I your long lost son?"

It was getting complicated and I was thinking, "What have I done?" What if she didn't want to talk to me? How would I handle rejection at this time in my life? What happens now if Juanita calls back and says my birth mother has passed on? My mind was going a mile a minute with all these crazy thoughts going through my head.

The phone rang three times before I could pick it up. I knew that this was it, that one way or another I would have an answer. It was Juanita.

"Hello," I said.

"Ed, I found your birth mother. She answered the phone. She has been worried about you all her life. She wants you to call her. She said that you might not want to talk to her."

She was wrong on that point. Indeed I was willing, able, and ready to talk to her even though I was trembling and not sure what I would say to her. After all it had been 57 years and we had a lot of catching up to do.

Before I called, Juanita told me that my birth mother stated she had pictures of me as a baby in the home where she stayed before and after my birth. She had kept those pictures close to her, hoping one day that she would be able to share them with me. I took a breath, said a prayer, and asked God to guide me as to what I was about to say to my birth mother.

It was September 14, 2004, between 12 noon and 1 p.m. when I dialed her number. She answered the telephone in the sweetest voice I have ever heard. I said, "Mrs. Virginia, I think you just had a call from my friend, Juanita White."

She replied, "Yes, I did."

Then I said, "I assume that I am your son."

She said, "Yes, you are. I have thought about you, cried about you, and wondered if you were having a good life."

Right about then I realized I was crying, and so was she. I was trying to hold it together, but I was not doing a good job of it.

The only thing that came out of my mouth was, "Mrs. Virginia, I've had a great life and I was raised well. If you would like to know what I have been doing with my life, go to my web site."

Can you believe that I find my birth mother and all I can do is send her to my web site? Well, I was at a loss for words. I told her that I would call her the next day. Both of us were filled with happiness, knowing how long she had waited to talk to her son. She gave birth to me on February 14, 1947. In my opinion, this was a blessing for her and for me.

Next, I called my wife at work. I said, "I just talked to my birth mother. I'll tell you the rest during family hour tonight." I could tell by her silence that she was stunned. She agreed and we hung up our phones. I called my daughter next at home and said, "I found my birth mother—family hour." She said, "OK."

Every day, Bernadette, Kendra, and I come home from work or wherever and have what we call family hour. We may or may not have cocktails, but we discuss what happened during the day while we were away from one another. It can include personal matters, family members, employment issues, or world interest conversations. We have laughed, cried, and prayed over the years during our family hour.

You can imagine what this day was like. When family hour came, mouths were wide open, and every detail had to be repeated two or three times. All the gathered documentation had to be reviewed again and all the questions asked and answered. All speculations surrounding the secret were opened like Pandora's Box, because there was a living breathing person, my birth mother, who knew the true story and was willing to talk about it.

The next day, September 15, 2004, after the initial shock of making contact, I called my birth mother again. We talked and she really made my head spin after she said to me, "You are the oldest child and you have two sisters and two brothers." All this time, I felt alone in the world thinking that I was an only child.

I asked her if she would welcome a visit from my family and me, and she answered, "Yes, I would." We set a date, October 9,

2004, to go to Dayton for our first visit since she last held me as a baby.

On Thursday, October 7, I had an exhibit and reception for Louisville's First Friday of the Month Gallery Hop. We had a great turn out for the first of this series of art exhibits, beginning with me and continuing with other local artists. On Friday, October 8, Bernadette, Kendra, and I started our journey to Dayton, stopping in Cincinnati where we spent the day at the newly opened Underground Railroad Museum. There, we were surprised to find a reference and a picture of my sculpture, *Spirit of Freedom*. We left Cincinnati and continued on to Dayton, and checked into the Doubletree Hotel downtown at 6 p.m.

I got involved with more art that evening because Dayton was having their Gallery Hop night. My friend, Bing Davis, had recently renovated his private gallery and community workshop for children and adults, the Willis Bing Davis Art Gallery. He picked me up and I remained there until closing and then returned to the hotel.

I couldn't really sleep well because I was anticipating meeting my birth mother for the first time. I was up bright and early Saturday morning. I was somewhat apprehensive since I didn't know what to expect and how my new family would receive us. Bernadette didn't want us to arrive empty-handed. Always a Southern hostess, she suggested that we take or send flowers. Luckily, we found a florist who would deliver and the flowers arrived before we did.

We reached the house at about twelve o'clock and my birth mother's sister, my Aunt Myrt, met us at the door. My birth mother came out from the kitchen and we looked at each other and it was as if time stood still for several brief moments. Then we embraced and held each other for the longest time. The baby she had 57 years earlier had returned to her arms, reminding her of when she last held me. This time, I returned to her as a grown man. It was electric; it is a moment that I shall never forget. Two moments stand out for me—the day of our first phone call contact and our first meeting together with the Rakestraw and Revere family members all around us.

My brother, Kevin Rakestraw, a retired mortgage banker, came with his son Matthew from Detroit. My Uncle Gilbert Revere and his wife Ruth, their two granddaughters, and their son Todd arrived. My brother John is mentally disabled. He arrived with my sister Paula's son Rian.

*Our first meeting
after 57 years apart*

*My mother, brothers
and sisters: (l to r)
Kevin, Debbra, John
Paula, Ed, Mother*

The house was filled with smiling faces and greetings. After an hour of chitchat, they left and Bernadette, Kendra, and I were alone with my birth mother. We had asked to have some private time to ask questions and promised the family that we would meet them in an hour at the Community Center where they had set up for dinner and invited other relatives.

When we arrived at the Center, my sister Debbra was there. She works for Head Start and volunteers at the Parkside Recreation Center. We had plenty to eat and three full hours of fellowship. There was a banner with my name as well as Bernadette's and Kendra's names that welcomed us and expressed love for us.

(l to r) Aunt Myrtis Zoober, Uncle Gilbert Revere, and Mother

My birth mother is a loving, caring person who has carried the burden of not knowing what became of a son she had to leave behind at the foundling home. She told me that she had been drugged and sexually molested by her father, Ben Revere, over a period of time. She became pregnant, and that is why I had to be left at the home. Her father worked for a battery company and had a distinctive body odor. She had complained to her mother, Emma Elizabeth Smith Revere, that on some mornings that she smelled like her father, but she didn't know why. She didn't realize that she was pregnant, and it was her mother who informed her of what had happened.

From the beginning, Virginia's mother and father had a troubled relationship. Her mother would often leave her father and go to live with her parents. Whenever they went to Family Court, my birth mother took on the responsibility of trying to keep their family together. The courts wanted her to decide which parent to live with and she would always answer, "Both of my parents."

Unbelievably, she was able to stay with me at the Home for six months. She was really supposed to leave after I was born. At 15 years old, she was the youngest woman living in a dormitory, with others from Cincinnati, Dayton, and Louisville. The staff taught her how to knit and to crochet, something that she continues today because it was her connection to me. She said that her greatest moments were to sneak in the nursery to hold me in my arms and care for me, and that I was a peaceful baby. Her saddest moment was having to leave me behind to move on with her life.

The only reason we would think of for her being able to stay six months rather than six days is the fact that every afternoon she would play the piano for the ladies who ran the Home. She was a distinguished piano player with plans to become a concert pianist Aunt Myrt and Uncle Gilbert remember going to visit Virginia in the Home.

She returned to her family home to finish her junior year of high school and help take care of her mother, brothers, and sisters.

Virginia Revere married Mr. John Paul Rakestraw on June 28, 1952, and he was the father of my siblings. The title of a newspaper article by Valryn Bush for the *Dayton Daily News* in 1994 described her as "Dayton's own 'angel of mercy.' Virginia Rakestraw spent 25 years working at the YWCA in Dayton, starting out as a volunteer and retiring as a Director and Chairwoman at the DeSoto Bass YWCA. She had persuaded the YWCA Board of Directors to approve a residence program with inexpensive housing for single women in 1979. In 1982, she persuaded the Y's Board to provide rooms for homeless women who could not pay their rent, and the emergency housing program was started. She networked with United Way, the Salvation Army, Montgomery County Community Action Agency, and Family Service Association, for medical care, counseling, and housing for these women.

We now talk on the phone weekly. We have written I don't know how many letters to each other and I also write to my brothers and sisters. When I look at them I see a reflection of myself through our birth mother. I now have a host of nieces, nephews, aunts, and an uncle—a whole new family to share with the world.

The good news is that they knew about me all along. My birth mother has always kept me present in their lives. They knew I existed before I knew about them. How do I feel now that I have found Virginia? I feel blessed and I believe my life is whole and complete now that I know who I am and where I come from—strong stock, Revere stock.

I know that my birth mother was under a lot of pressure and carried a lot of baggage on her shoulders for a long time. I know that she has always prayed that someday this dream would come true. I am thankful that she wanted to see and talk to me after all those years and that her children and family members welcomed my family and me.

I had prayed to know the truth of my birth. Any sadness of this story is outweighed by the fact that I am alive and my birth mother is happy.

One of the first questions I asked my birth mother is why she didn't try to find me. She had seen shows on television that showed that often such a search didn't end happily. She decided that she had made a decision 57 years ago, though not of her choosing, and hoped the best for me wherever I was.

If genes are important, they show up in different ways. Both she and I work with our hands, we have compassion for others, and we correspond with letters. It seems ironic to me that she was designing dresses and teaching young women to sew and become self-sufficient at the YWCA while I was making bronze monuments. The year that I graduated from art school, 1969, she was graduating from Opals School of Custom Design and Pattern Making.

She used to sell Mary Kay Cosmetics and was at a Mary Kay convention in Detroit, where she saw the *Joe Louis* statue that I had created in 1987. She and several of her associates stood admiring it; now she says that she should have had a feeling that it was created by me. I had to smile at her comment because I know mothers' think differently when it involves their children. What a irony it was that while we were in and out of Detroit, I had a brother living there and didn't even know it.

It is wonderful to hear from my brother, Kevin. We look alike, we both talk a lot, and Virginia says we walk alike. Kevin and I have exchanged bets on basketball games, and when I gave him a challenge and a point spread for the Cincinnati versus University of Louisville game, I won the bet. Kevin had to go all the way to Florida to a golf tournament before he a found a bottle of Woodford Reserve bourbon to pay off the bet. I can tell you right now, that was one lucky bet which I probably could not place again.

As Maya Angelou would say, my birth mother and my mom who adopted me are two phenomenal women. I thank God for them both, but most of all I thank God for the gift of life. I thank God for all of my family in Louisville, as well as my Dayton family. I will always be grateful for the love that my birth mother held in her heart for me for all these years.

What a wonderful journey this has been. To be able to share it with you and the rest of the world is even more special. My advice to those who have read this portion of the book and who may be searching for a loved one is just take your time. It's a lot of work and requires patience because you will have to wait for information. Do your research and put your trust in God for He will see you through. I feel my soul has been set free and the secrets have ended. I love you Mama, and I love you Virginia, my birth mother.

This portion of the book could not have been written without the love and support of three special people—Bernadette, my wife of 38 years; my friend, Juanita L. White, who helped to guide me through the whole process; and LaVerne Shumake Dunning, who helped research the genealogy and family history of the Hamilton and Revere families. Special thanks are due my birth mother, Virginia Rakestraw, for the gift of life and carrying me in her heart for over fifty years. I thank all of you.

Finally, I quote from a card sent from Virginia to Juanita, "My dear Juanita, There are no words to express my thanks to you for bringing me such overwhelming joy. Now my soul can rest. You will forever be in my prayers. Love in Christ, Virginia Rakestraw."

ADDENDUM

IF I HAD TO DO IT ALL OVER AGAIN

There are some things that I think are just predestined or ordained. Even if I had the chance, I wouldn't change anything. The stars were aligned for this young boy to do the things that he is doing and has done. I believe it was my destiny; it just may have been a blessing that the circumstances of my birth turned out the way they did.

All things happen for a reason, and I can only thank God for my loving and caring family in Louisville who raised me and made sure that I didn't want for anything. Having the love of my extended Louisville family members for support has been a blessing. Being able to enjoy the gift of life from my birth mother is more than a blessing.

Having great art teachers throughout my school years who worked with me to develop my artistic abilities gave me the start I needed to maintain an art career. Being exposed to all facets of art during my college years opened my mind to unlimited possibilities.

The Louisville Art Workshop impacted and provided necessary encouragement to help launch my career. Had my graduation show at the Art Center School been displayed during the normal month-long run, my association with the Louisville Art Workshop may not have occurred until some time later.

Above all, I truly believe that meeting Barney Bright put me in the right place at the right time. Had I not taken advantage of that opportunity, I wouldn't be doing what I am doing today.

My life has come full circle, I am whole, knowing who I am, where I come from, and not afraid to continue my life's journey.

NO MATTER HOW BIG OR SMALL

I love to create lasting works of art that commemorate people and events in history. But more and more I think it is the process of sculpting that interests me the most. When I am not working on large-scale projects, I enjoy working on plaques.

VIC HELLARD, JR.

When I was asked to make a plaque for the late Vic Hellard, Jr., I was given a photograph and background information about the long-time director of the Kentucky Legislative Research Commission.

I was also told that when he went to his office in the State Capitol building, he always had his track shoes on. This fact helped me when I created the 24 by 36 inch plaque.

I started with his likeness and placed the state Capitol building behind him. At the bottom, I modeled some track shoes and added a statement that he made in 1995: "We are told that government is the enemy and the government does not exist outside ourselves. The plain fact is we are the government."

The bronze plaque was unveiled on April 12, 2000, in the State Capitol rotunda in Frankfort, Kentucky. It is mounted outside the third-floor office where Hellard presided over the Commission staff for eighteen years.

DR. THOMAS CLARK

Dr. Thomas Clark was Kentucky's most prominent historian. He worked tirelessly as a scholar, teacher, researcher, conservationist, and preservationist.

Clark not only studied Kentucky history, he also saved part of it when he stopped the state librarian, who ran out of storage space, from selling truckloads of state records as scrap in 1936.

Just as Clark saved state records, I salvaged the actual clay model that I used to make his plaque, because I did not have the heart to tear it up. I usually recycle used clay, but his clay plaque was left intact and is now in my studio.

A 24 by 36 inch plaque was originally created with an image of Dr. Clark and the Kentucky History Center behind him and was dedicated in April, 2001. This center was renamed the Thomas D. Clark Center for Kentucky History on July 9, 2005, in Frankfort. The final version of the plaque was changed to depict Dr. Clark looking down on the Kentucky History Center, since he was the guiding light behind its construction and operation. Dr. Clark died in June, 2005.

DAVID ROBERT LEWIS

Purdue University officials asked me to create a plaque of David Robert Lewis, who in 1894 was the first African American to graduate with a Bachelor's Degree from Purdue University's Civil Engineering School. The committee brought a picture of him to my studio for me to use to create his likeness. When I looked at the picture, I told them that I had seen Mr. Lewis before.

They said, "No, you haven't seen this man. You don't know this man."

I replied, "Yes, I do."

Lewis was a professor at Hampton Institute. The committee didn't know I was connected to Hampton via the *Booker T. Washington* statue and happened to have a Hampton photographic essay book from the 1800s. The first time I had looked through the book, the photo of a dapper-looking man teaching an engineering class grabbed my attention.

Now, I went to my bookcase, got the book, and said, "Is this David Lewis?"

The response was, "I'll be damned."

I'd looked at him all along and did not know that one day I would make an 24 by 36 inch bronze plaque memorializing him. The plaque of David Robert Lewis (1861-1929) was dedicated February 12, 2000, at Purdue University.

WHITNEY M. YOUNG, JR. MEMORIAL

I enjoy shining the light on people who have not been adequately recognized for their impact on humanity. Whitney M. Young, Jr., is one such person. While other civil rights leaders chose to spark social change through protests, marches, and demonstrations, Whitney Young chose another route. He took his skills to America's boardrooms. He sat in on strategy sessions and negotiated for equal access to quality employment, education, housing, health care, and social services.

Whitney, an alumnus of Kentucky State University (KSU), served as president of the National Urban League from 1961 until his death in 1971. KSU's Alumni Association commissioned the *Whitney M. Young, Jr.* Memorial. I began working on the project while I was finishing *The Spirit of Freedom*.

I had to work on the statue of Whitney Young at another studio a few miles away from my own, since the *Spirit of Freedom* and the statue both couldn't fit in my studio at the same time. It threw me totally off because I just could not get used to working every day in a space that was not mine. My dust wasn't in there and my stuff wasn't in there, but I was on a deadline.

The bronze statue of Whitney M. Young, Jr. is slightly larger than life size and sits atop a five-foot base on the campus of Kentucky State University in Frankfort. It was dedicated on October 9, 1998.

MEDGAR WILEY EVERS LIFE-SIZE BUST

The legacy of Medgar Wiley Evers' life is present everywhere, especially in Mississippi. He was the first field secretary of the NAACP in Mississippi during the difficult times between 1954 and 1963.

This peaceful man, whose life was detailed in the film *Ghosts of Mississippi,* constantly implored others that violence was not the way to win their goals. He was killed in 1963 because of his work in civil rights. His death helped galvanize the national voter-rights movement. Many tributes have been paid to Medgar Evers over the years, and I am proud to have been a part of this one.

In 1998, General Mills, Inc. commissioned me to create a life-size portrait bronze bust of Evers. The bust was unveiled at the NAACP National Convention in Baltimore, Maryland, on July 9, 2000.

LENNY LYLES LIFE-SIZE STATUE

It was an honor to be chosen to create sculptures of local and national people of prominence. Lenny Lyles is one of Louisville's outstanding citizens, both as an athlete and businessman.

Lyles starred as a running back and defensive back for the University of Louisville from 1954 through 1957. Following graduation, the National Football League's Baltimore Colts drafted him in the first round. A member of the University of Louisville Athletic Hall of Fame, Lyles followed his NFL career with an equally successful career in private business.

I was commissioned by philanthropist Owsley Brown Frazier to produce a life-size bronze statue of Lyles. Because he was known as the "Fastest Man in Football" during his college heyday, my representational piece shows him in a sprinter's stance.

The sculpture was unveiled on October 12, 2000, on the grounds of the Cardinal Park complex on the University of Louisville campus.

MIGRATION TO THE WEST

The dedication of *York* on the Belvedere in downtown Louisville was also the beginning of a new commission. This work was the second commission I created for Owsley Brown Frazier. This statue was for his new museum, the Frazier Historical Arms Museum, at 9th and Main Streets.

Two world class collections joined forces in this museum—those of Frazier and the Royal Armory of London. The Frazier Museum deals with artistry, technology, exploration, and humanity as it all relates to the weapons used through the centuries. I was

Clay model for
Migration to the West,
2003

commissioned to design a bronze sculpture for the main lobby. The *Migration to the West* was born through the efforts of my team of artists, including C. Robert Markert, my friend and assistant; Forest Boone, president of Museumrock Products who designed the base; and my assistant Tamina Karem.

The statue is a life-size depiction of a frontier family, standing tall and looking west toward their future as they migrate to a new frontier. Life on the plains was not easy, as this family—a mother, a father, three children, and their little dog—endured dangers and the unknown that faced many families searching for a new way of life.

Putting on the base

During installation of this statue, we almost had a catastrophe. My friend, the sculptor Paul Fields, and his assistant Al Nelson, were charged with placing the statue on its base, which had been placed in the lobby of the museum the night before.

The bronze family, weighing approximately 1800 pounds, was brought through the front door. We had a lift to place the statue on the rock formation, which was about two feet high. As we were balancing the statue on the lift, Paul raised it to the height of the rock. The back end of the statue's two sides was on top of

Migration to the
West, *bronze, Frazier
Historical Arms
Museum, 2003*

the rock. As we were pushing the statue back toward the wall and
farther on the rock, the statue started to tilt forward and drop down.
My first instinct was to run, but the seven people were able to hold
it as Paul quickly hit the up button on the lift and the statue slid
into place.

Migration to the West now greets visitors to the museum as they
enter the front lobby.

WORKS FROM 1970 TO 2004

EARLY WORKS

*Untitled bronze
female form, private
collection,
Washington, D.C.,
1976*

Embryo, cast
*aluminum,
private collection,
Louisville, KY 1976*

Mother and Child,
clay, private collection,
KY, 1975

The Four Horsemen of
the Apocalypse, *bronze,*
private collection,
Winchester, KY, 1978

St. Frances of Rome, *bronze, St. Frances of Rome Catholic Church, Louisville, KY, 1979*

Side view

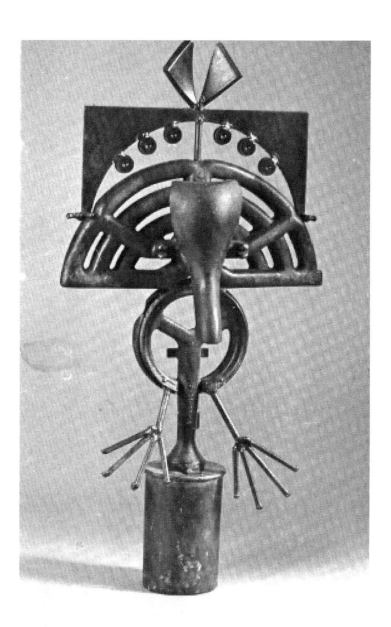

Bird Form, Junkology
Series, *welded metal,
private collection,
Louisville, KY, 1979*

Totem, Confinement
Series, *metal
fabrication, collection
of artist, 1980 (photo
by Kenneth Hayden)*

Brother Can You
Spare a Dime?
Confinement
Series, *mixed media
collage, private
collection, Nashville,
TN, 1980*

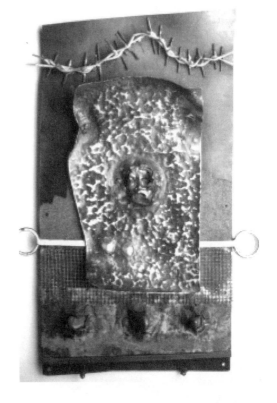

Crown of Thorns,
Confinement
Series, *mixed media,
private collection, 1980*

Nile Mother, *mixed
media, Atlanta Life
Insurance Co., Atlanta,
GA, 1986*

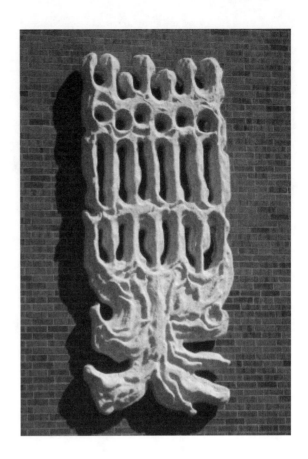

Menorah Tree of
Life, *cast stone (ten
feet by eighteen feet by
one foot), The Temple,
Louisville, KY, (in
collaboration with C.
Robert Markert)
1986*

Joe Louis, *polychrome
plaster, estate of
Wendell Cherry,
Louisville, KY, 1986*

Ed Hamilton

RECENT WORKS

Sengbe Pieh *from* The
Amistad Memorial,
plaster, metal, & wood,
collection of the Speed
Art Museum, Louisville,
KY, 1992 (photo by
Kenneth Hayden)

Detail of Sengbe Pieh *from* The Amistad Memorial, *plaster, metal, & wood, collection of the Speed Art Museum, Louisville, KY, 1992 (photo by Kenneth Hayden)*

Sengbe Pieh, *plaster study for* The Amistad Memorial, *collection of the Speed Art Museum, Louisville, 1991*

Spirit of Freedom
*marquette, #1 of a
limited edition of
100, bronze on black
marble, collection of
the artist, 1998*

*Untitled studies, cast
from* The Spirit of
Freedom *mold, #1 of a
limited edition of 25,
bronze on limestone,
owned by Anthony
French, Louisville, KY,
1998*

Untitled study, cast from The Spirit of Freedom *mold, #1 of a limited edition of 25, bronze on limestone, owned by Anthony French, Louisville, KY, 1998*

Untitled study, cast from
The Spirit of Freedom
*mold, #1 of a limited
edition of 25, bronze on
limestone, collection of
the Speed Art Museum,
Louisville, KY, 1998*

Whitney M. Young,
Jr., *plaster study for
life-size bronze,
collection of the artist,
2000*

Frederick Douglass,
*plaster study for life-size
bronze, collection of the
artist, 2004*